SKIPPING NOT TRIPPING

HOW TO HELP CHILDREN WHOSE MOTOR SKILLS SEEM CLUMSY AND UNCOORDINATED

SKIPPING NOT TRIPPING

HOW TO HELP CHILDREN WHOSE MOTOR SKILLS SEEM CLUMSY AND UNCOORDINATED

Neralie Cocks

SIMON & SCHUSTER
AUSTRALIA

NOTE: The pronouns 'he' and 'she' have been alternated throughout the chapters of this book.

SKIPPING NOT TRIPPING: HOW TO HELP CHILDREN WHOSE MOTOR SKILLS SEEM CLUMSY AND UNCOORDINATED

First published in Australasia in 1992 by
Simon & Schuster Australia
20 Barcoo Street, East Roseville NSW 2069

A Paramount Communications Company
Sydney New York London Toronto Tokyo Singapore

National Library of Australia
Cataloguing in Publication data

Cocks, Neralie.
Skipping not tripping: how to help children whose motor skills seem clumsy and uncoordinated

Bibliography.
Includes index.
ISBN 0 7318 0304 3.

1. Motor ability in children. 2. Motor learning. 3. Clumsiness.
I. Title.

152.334

Cover illustration by Roger Roberts
Cover design by Christie & Eckermann
Designed by Kathie Baxter Smith/Design Smiths
Typeset in Australia by Asset Typesetting Pty. Ltd.
Printed in Australia by Australian Print Group

FOREWORD

It may not seem such a big deal to be a bit clumsy but it still leaves many children feeling inferior. Children with coordination problems are not helped when those around them can see nothing but their weakness, and no one notices all their untapped skills and potential.

This is a positive book written by a highly experienced, hands-on therapist — Neralie Cocks. I have been a great supporter of Neralie's work for years. She has a certain magic as she helps children, quickly turning the focus from failure to success. Therapy to her means daily activities that feel like fun. She is a realist, doing what is necessary and not going overboard. Neralie recognises that clumsy children may also have difficulties with behaviour, inattention and specific learning weaknesses. She looks past any problem, to see how life can be lived to the full.

This book is about making the most of our given strengths and weaknesses, then getting on with life in a confident way. If your child is **tripping not skipping** read on — things are about to change!

Dr Christopher Green
Author of *Toddler Taming* and *Babies!*
Specialist Paediatrician
Head of the Child Development Unit,
The Children's Hospital (The Royal Alexandra Hospital)
Sydney

To the therapists of the
Royal Alexandra Hospital for Children,
Camperdown.

CONTENTS

ACKNOWLEDGEMENTS

I would like to thank Dr Christopher Green (Head, Child Development Unit) and Dr Paul Hutchins (Staff Physician) both of the Royal Alexandra Hospital for Children, for their advice, support and encouragement in the production of this book. To Dr Christopher Green, for his many helpful suggestions in the way that this subject be presented for the guidance of the general reader. To Dr Paul Hutchins, for his interest and practical help especially during the early stages.

Everyone looks for pictures and illustrations in a book. When dealing with children's motor difficulties, illustrations can portray at a glance what is being said in the text. I believe that the illustrations of Carol Dunn have helped enormously in conveying my message.

Thank you to my occupational therapy colleagues, Sally Brown, Elizabeth Bardos, Maria Passarello, Mary-Anne Bonney and also June Straw and Betina Fratzia (Hornsby Hospital) for their suggestions, and to those parents who helped read the earlier drafts.

I would like to thank the management and staff of the Royal Alexandra Hospital for Children for their support. In particular, Nikki Brown (Media Manager) who encouraged me to develop my original thoughts on the subject into this book. Also, Lorraine Partington for introducing me to the mysteries and usefulness of word processing and to Kate Watson for her moral support and suggestions for resource material.

Many thanks to my friend, Rosemary Harle for reading the manuscript and making suggestions regarding the style and presentation, and to Kirsty Melville and Narelle Segecic of Simon & Schuster Australia for their enthusiasm and guidance in the final production.

Finally, many thanks to my dear mother who supported me with innumerable cups of tea, and encouraged me when I felt like giving up.

Neralie Cocks
May 1992

INTRODUCTION

'Motor skills' are a part of your child's everyday life. They comprise the basic movement abilities such as running, skipping, catching and throwing balls, riding a bike, using scissors, holding pencils and writing. *Skipping not Tripping* is for parents of primary school children who find motor skills such as these difficult to master. It will show you how to help improve your child's ability, confidence and therefore enjoyment in performing these skills.

All of us differ from each other in our motor abilities. Some, like the instructor of an aerobics class, are at one end of the spectrum of motor ability. At the other end, is the poorly coordinated person who avoids sporting activities at all costs. And, in between these two extremes, are those capable of a range of motor abilities. People's level of confidence in performing these skills can be observed even within an aerobics class. The well-coordinated are usually positioned in the front of the class. At the back, there are often one or two who find it hard to coordinate arms and legs together with style. Even though they participate in and enjoy the class, they often prefer to remain unobserved.

As adults we have the option to steer clear of tasks which embarrass us or are difficult. Children do not have the same freedom of choice.

Life can be stressful for children with motor difficulties because so much of the primary school day revolves around motor-based activities, both in the classroom and in the playground. It can be upsetting to see children struggling to keep up with their peers, only to be rejected because they cannot catch a ball, or run and climb like the other kids. They often feel disheartened because they are last to be picked for a team and often are left standing alone on the sideline.

It is believed that at least five per cent of children who attend regular primary school have significant motor difficulties. This affects their ability to participate in physically active games, school work, and even self-care tasks like dressing and eating tidily. Being different, being unable to join in and keep up, can easily injure these children's self-esteem.

As a parent, you may be a little concerned about your child's motor development, or alternatively you may be acutely worried and frustrated by limited resources and lack of information. This book aims to guide you through both these areas, by providing an overview of motor development, by showing you how motor difficulties manifest and by telling you what positive steps you as parents can take.

Skipping not Tripping is a self-help book offering many practical ideas and suggestions which you can try at home. It is not only instructive but will also provide enjoyment for you and your child. Of course if you need more information, then you should see a paediatric occupational therapist or physiotherapist.

It is important to realise that therapists do not possess a 'magic wand' which can turn a clumsy and uncoordinated child into an Olympic athlete. What is important is that these children experience success and achievement rather than feelings of failure, rejection and loss of confidence.

The ideas and activities contained in this book have been gathered from my experience as an occupational therapist, from other therapists, parents and of course the children themselves. I have tried to illustrate, in a practical way, the needs of these children and how best to meet them. I hope you find *Skipping not Tripping* an encouraging book.

CHAPTER 1

'CLUMSY AND UNCOORDINATED IN MOTOR SKILLS': WHAT DOES IT MEAN?

Every parent wants their child to be able to successfully participate in sport, leisure and school work. When children's motor difficulties make it hard for them to keep up with their peers, they might need some extra help to guide them through their developing years.

In this chapter the words 'clumsy' and 'uncoordinated' are explained. These words are often used to describe children who are not good at perfecting their motor skills and who may look a bit clumsy and uncoordinated in their attempts at physical activities. We look at those children who are at risk of developing motor difficulties, and guidance is given on when you should seek an opinion and who to see if you are concerned about your child's motor development.

AREN'T ALL CHILDREN CLUMSY AND UNCOORDINATED AT TIMES?

Yes, all children may be described as 'clumsy' and 'uncoordinated' at some stage in their motor development. Consider the jerky movements of an infant when first attempting to reach and grasp a rattle, or the constant falls and tumbles of the toddler learning to walk. Older children learning to ride a bike look clumsy in their attempts to coordinate balance and timing with pushing bicycle pedals ... so what exactly do we mean by the words 'clumsy and uncoordinated'?

Children who cannot complete or perform a motor task that they want to do, in a smooth and successful manner appropriate for their age, may appear clumsy and uncoordinated. Their quality of movement and the speed at which they learn a new skill such as riding a bike, swimming, drawing or writing differ from most children of similar age.

Children are required to master a wide and diverse range of motor skills. Large body movements are referred to as **'gross motor skills'**, and include running and jumping. Hand and finger movements are referred to as **'fine motor skills'**, and include sewing and writing.

For some children, every motor task involving gross or fine movements can cause major difficulties. Even the muscles associated with talking, chewing and swallowing can be poorly coordinated, resulting in lack of fluency in speech and eating difficulties. Not all children with motor problems, however, have difficulties in all these areas. For some, the problem may be confined to fine motor skills, particularly writing. Other children may have difficulty with total body movements and coordination of larger muscle groups, and yet be quite proficient in fine manipulative movements. Others may easily fall, trip or knock things over. As we can see, there is enormous variation in the way that clumsiness and poor coordination can affect the daily lives of these children.

Due to this enormous variation of motor performance, it is confusing and difficult for doctors, therapists, teachers and psychologists to develop a single diagnostic word to describe children who are having problems in the area of gross and fine motor skills development. As a result, a vast array of terminology is used, each focusing on the more specific aspects of the overall problem. You may have already come across some of these terms; they include: 'difficulties in perceptual-motor skills', 'visual-motor integration', 'visual-spatial skills', 'motor planning difficulties', 'dyspraxia', 'developmental coordination disorder', 'sensory motor problems', 'poor eye-hand/foot coordination', 'poor body awareness', 'poor gross and fine motor skills' and 'motor learning difficulties'. So as you can see, the list is just as diverse as the motor skills themselves!

Motor abilities vary between children — for some it is more difficult.

The words 'clumsiness' and 'uncoordinated' are used by doctors and therapists to describe those children whose movement problems are not due to brain damage, nerve damage, muscle disorders, or other specific diseases. In other words, these children are normal and healthy kids.

'Clumsy' and 'uncoordinated' worry some parents, as these words may seem somewhat critical and negative. They are however very general terms, describing children who tend to be messy and disorganised and who lack a smooth flow of movement. If we get bogged down in alternative and technical terminology, we are at risk of losing sight of the difficulties facing these children. No matter what you call the condition, life can be very frustrating for these children as they strive to meet the demands of classroom activities and keep up with their friends, brothers, sisters and cousins in physically active games.

WHO IS AT RISK OF HAVING MOTOR DIFFICULTIES?

For the vast majority of clumsy children, there is no known cause of motor difficulty. Some children, however, seem more at risk if there is a history of prematurity. Sometimes there is a family history of clumsiness, with children being remarkably like their parents. Parents may find their own child's motor difficulties particularly upsetting if they stumbled through their own school years.

There are different levels of clumsiness, sometimes reflecting different causes and problems.

Motor difficulties in some children may reflect an overall developmental immaturity which usually improves with time as their bodies mature. These children take a little longer to acquire age appropriate motor skills. However, once they achieve these skills, they can perform them without appearing clumsy or uncoordinated. The suggestions in this book are appropriate for these children because they provide a wide range of challenging activities which help develop their motor skills to the optimum.

A significant number of clumsy children are 'disorganised'

in their development: they may have poor concentration and memory, are dreamy, fidgety and impulsive. Children who have an in-built difficulty in concentration are usually diagnosed as having an Attention Deficit Disorder, with or without hyperactivity (see Appendix I). They may forget where they have put things, take ages to pack their bags and get ready for school, dress carelessly, eat messily and end up looking a disaster before they put one foot out the front door. Such children usually present with a 'package' of problems, including learning difficulties, behaviour problems, speech and language difficulties, as well as clumsiness and poor coordination. Their problems may be evident in the preschool years, although difficulties usually manifest themselves as school gets harder and more demanding.

Some children may have difficulty attaining motor milestones because they are slow in all aspects of their development and their potential to develop normally is limited. Children with a demonstrable abnormality, or disease of the nervous system or muscles, may be given medical diagnoses such as cerebral palsy. These children's motor difficulties are very different from that of ordinary clumsiness and poor coordination. They require more specific exercises and individualised therapy programs which are different from the suggested activities in this book.

WHEN SHOULD I SEEK HELP AND WHERE DO I GO?

If your child seems clumsy and poorly coordinated for his age, he should be checked out medically. Your doctor, the medical officer at the local child health centre or a paediatrician are the people you should see. What you want is a professional opinion to exclude specific medical disorders, to ensure your child's vision and hearing are normal, and to organise appropriate help. Referral to therapy services should occur if your child's difficulties are significant enough to affect everyday functioning, both at home and school. Occupational therapists and physiotherapists have an important role to play in helping your child. As a surprising number of children also have language difficulties, speech pathologists are often involved.

Once your child is referred to a specialist, paediatric occupational therapists and physiotherapists will usually assess your child's motor ability by obtaining a history of the areas of difficulty and from observing the child's motor skills. Then, if therapy programs are needed, these will be provided on either an individual or group basis.

Occupational therapists are skilled at assessing children whose disorganisation, clumsiness and poor coordination affects their gross and fine motor skills, including their writing, playing and self-care abilities. Physiotherapists are skilled at assessing the quality of a child's movements, including their walking and running, as well as posture, muscle strength and tone. Occupational therapists and physiotherapists work closely together to help children with motor difficulties. Usually, physiotherapists focus on gross motor skills while occupational therapists focus on fine motor skills.

The chapters in this book which provide you with ideas on what can be done at home are very general. If possible, try and get in touch with local therapy services. It is difficult doing the activities, gauging progress and change by yourself, in isolation — without support and encouragement to modify what best to do as your child changes.

Therapists will monitor your child's progress and give guidance on the most appropriate activities to do at home. Occupational therapists, physiotherapists and speech pathologists who specialise in seeing children are usually based in hospitals, community health centres or in private practice (see Appendix III).

KEY POINTS

1. The terms 'clumsy and uncoordinated' refer to those children who cannot complete or perform a motor task in a smooth, mature and successful manner. These children stand out as different from others of their age.
2. If you are at all concerned about clumsiness and poor coordination in your child, see your family doctor or paediatrician.
3. Occupational therapists and physiotherapists have an important role to play in helping children who have difficulties in their motor skills. Therapy helps children gain confidence and improve their motor skills to the best of their ability.

CHAPTER 2

GROWING AND GAINING: AN OVERVIEW OF MOTOR DEVELOPMENT

In this chapter we look at the stages which children pass through to gain increasing competence in motor skills. To help your child with her motor difficulties, it is important that you understand normal motor development — otherwise you might place unrealistic expectations upon your child. As adults, we frequently make the mistake of expecting children to successfully achieve tasks which are too advanced for their age. This can only add further stress and unhappiness to those of our children who may be already having difficulties. An understanding of what skills are expected at certain ages, will help pinpoint areas of weakness and establish which need the most help within the framework of realistic expectations.

MOTOR DEVELOPMENT

Moving and the control of movement commences at birth and continues throughout life. At each developmental stage we expect our children to have acquired certain skills. Some of these come naturally, others need to be learnt. For example, babies do not need to be taught how to lift and turn their heads or roll over, toddlers do not need to be instructed on how to walk. Such motor skills come naturally, as if 'programed'. These in-built motor skills are the 'building blocks' for the more complex learnt motor skills developed in primary school years, such as playing the piano, ballet and swimming. The following 'thumb-nail' sketch will provide you with an opportunity to see how this progression occurs through the main stages of your child's development.

INFANCY AND EARLY CHILDHOOD: THE FIRST FIVE YEARS

The first five years of your child's life reveals a dramatic rate of acceleration in the development of motor skills.

The first 12 months is the most dramatic period of change: compare the dependency of your newborn baby to those skills she had achieved by her first birthday. It is a period of exploration through the senses of hearing, vision, touch and smell. Your baby initially turns her head towards sound, starts following faces and objects and then reaches out towards the source of sound, movement or colour. At first, her arm movements are uncoordinated, gradually becoming more on target and refined. She is then able to grasp hold of objects, feel different textures and shapes, and eventually control the opening of her fingers to release objects. Through many exploratory movements, she discovers her own body, and learns how to judge distances and control the speed and timing of her movements. By her first birthday, she can hold, bite and chew a biscuit, hold onto a cup or spoon, and even help 'unwrap' her birthday present.

Antigravity muscles are developing, so that by twelve months, she can crawl, stand and even take some steps.

At 18 months she can walk reliably without too much help as her antigravity muscles become stronger. She has learnt to judge distances, and is aware of her own body in relationship to objects and people; she can now negotiate around furniture and adults. She has learnt that if she stands up too quickly when under the coffee table, a bump on the head is the result. She can control her body movements; now it is easy for her to pick up a toy from a squatting position and to stand, meanwhile regaining balance. Once her gross motor development is underway, your toddler's energy can focus on finer movements. By eighteen months, she can stack a few blocks, help turn the pages of a book, pick up and place tiny objects, and even hold a pencil and scribble.

Your two-year-old can walk well and is ready to commence running — this is when life becomes fun for parents! She has developed balance and appreciation of distance to the extent that she now attempts to walk up stairs holding onto a rail. She has learnt to push a small tricycle with her feet, as well as steer, stop and start with control. Your two-year-old can even walk backwards while pulling a wheeled toy attached to a string. She can hold a pencil using thumb and fingers and is able to scribble round and round as well as imitating a vertical stroke. She can feed herself successfully with a spoon, drink independently from a cup, and replace the cup back on the table. Her early dressing skills are emerging, such as putting on shoes and a hat.

Your three-year-old can walk independently up and down stairs in an adult manner, jump off the bottom step with two feet together, and ride a tricycle using pedals. She can walk, stand, and run on tiptoes, and she can throw, catch, bounce and kick a ball. She can eat with spoon and fork, and is able to dress except for buttons, tight clothing and fastenings on shoes. She can thread beads, hold a pencil like an adult, copy a circle, draw mummy and daddy with some features and body parts. At three, she is able to manipulate and cut with scissors.

At four years of age, she is able to run up and down stairs, enjoy climbing ladders and trees and is most proficient at riding a tricycle with pedals. She has also developed sufficient balance to hop on one foot. Your four-year-old can draw human figures with their head, trunk, legs and sometimes arms and fingers. She can draw other pictures as well, for example, a simple house. She can manage brushing her teeth with supervision, wiping herself after using the toilet, and dressing/undressing herself except for hard to reach buttons, bows and shoelaces.

Five-year-olds are ready for school. At this stage, your child can skip and move rhythmically to music, can hop on either leg, and maintain her balance while walking along a line or a low balance beam. She can thread large needles and make attempts at sewing. She may be able to copy a square, triangle and even write letters. Her drawings are more sophisticated, showing recognisable people with head, trunk, legs, arms and facial features. Her 'houses' are more detailed and include windows, doors, curtains, etc. Her scissor skills have improved, so now she can cut along a line and cut out simple shapes. She is able to use a knife and fork together, dress and undress alone — though doing up shoelaces can still be a bit of a challenge.

In Summary:

1. Infancy and early childhood is the major growth period in the development of your child's motor skills.
2. It is when the in-built foundations for motor development are laid: looking, feeling, touching, listening, reaching, grasping, timing movements, developing antigravity muscles, balance and body awareness.

3. It is a period where your child's natural motor abilities lead on to more sophisticated and learnt motor skills such as cutting with scissors, using cutlery, drawing.

MIDDLE CHILDHOOD: THE FIVE- TO EIGHT-YEAR-OLD

This is the period when relationships with other children are important. Games and physical activities are the primary focus. Children at this age are constantly on the move — just observe the school playground at lunch time. This is when children learn about the rules of games, and that to be accepted into a group, one needs to follow and obey the rules. Motor skills are becoming refined; both in gross and fine motor abilities.

During the middle childhood period, your child has moved away from riding tricycles to riding two-wheeler bikes. In the swimming pool, he is able to progress from dog paddling to learning the arm movements in freestyle while kicking. Between six and eight, your child becomes more skilled at tossing, bouncing, throwing and sometimes successfully catching tennis balls. He is beginning to learn how to handle a cricket bat, play soccer, and enjoy rough and tumble games. Balance has become further refined; now he can walk along fences and brick walls. It is the period when your child may commence piano, ballet lessons and other skilled interests.

This is a time of learning to write words and short sentences with letters gradually getting smaller, well-spaced and fairly uniform in alignment. Around eight years of age, your child's drawings are beginning to show perspective, and action figures can be drawn in reasonable proportion.

He can cut out irregular shapes, paste accurately and even manage to use sticky tape to fix things. He can fully dress and undress himself, is capable of brushing and combing his hair in an organised way, and has the skills to scrub and file his finger nails and clean his teeth properly. He may have problems with the school tie, but can now manage shoelaces!

In Summary:
1. During middle childhood, keeping up with other children in physically active games, understanding the rules and making friends is important.
2. Children at this age are usually fully independent in self-care.
3. The ability to write words and sentences emerges at this age.

LATE CHILDHOOD: THE NINE- TO TWELVE-YEAR-OLD

During the late childhood period, the acquisition of new motor skills is not as rapid as in the previous stages. It is, however, the time of perfecting and refining skilled motor development. Children are far more adventurous on their bikes and have better control of speed. Their ball skills are more accurate, and now they are able to throw and catch tennis balls with accuracy and participate successfully in games such as handball. Children of this age have more stamina and enjoy outdoor activities such as bushwalking, camping, surfing, fishing and exploring their surroundings with friends.

By the age of nine to twelve, your child is more adept with fine motor tasks. She is able to use tools such as saws, hammers and can correctly grip the handles. Children of this age are capable of constructing simple woodwork projects, sewing and making simple garments.

The mechanics of handwriting are less laboured and more automatic. Your child is capable of writing in a straight line without lines to guide, her letter formation is smaller and she is aware of accurate spacing, setting out and punctuation. At school, she is required to undertake 'projects' which involve researching, being organised and being able to cut, paste and lay out material accurately.

Motor development is a process where new skills are not only gained but refined.

At this age, your child is acutely aware of her own strengths and weaknesses, and of those of others. It is a time when she is selected onto teams because of her proficiency at motor skills. Friends and belonging to a group are important. She can easily feel rejected if she does not meet the standard and abilities of the 'group'.

In Summary:

1. Motor development for the nine- to twelve-year-old focuses on refining and perfecting both gross and fine motor skills.
2. Children commence undertaking more adult-type activities such as handling tools and sewing.
3. Children are at risk of being rejected by their peers if they do not meet the requirements of the group.

KEY POINTS

1. Understanding normal motor development helps parents develop realistic expectations and appreciate the difficulties their child may be experiencing.
2. Motor development is a process where new skills are gained and refined.
3. Skilled motor performance is learnt — it does not 'just happen'. Some children learn more easily than others, as not all children have the same in-built motor abilities.
4. Children are at risk of being rejected by their peers if they are unable to keep up in physically active games.

CHAPTER 3

FLUENT AND FLOWING MOVEMENTS: HOW DO WE DO IT?

What are the important factors necessary to achieve the smooth and well-timed movements which enable both adults and children to be successful in a wide range of daily activities? We have already looked at the motor skills appropriate for a child at each developmental stage. We will now consider more closely the underlying processes and contributing factors necessary to achieve those age-appropriate skills.

Most therapists would agree that the following areas are significant if a movement is to be 'fluent and flowing', in both the basic in-built motor skills and the more complex learnt skills. Each area has an important role to play if a movement and motor skill is to be performed with control and style. I like to compare it to the successful performance of a choir or orchestra. Both are made up of individual voices or instruments, singing or playing different notes but with the aim of blending together to produce a pleasing result. If just one of the voices or instruments is 'out of tune', the whole performance can be spoilt. So too with your child; if any one or more of the following areas are 'out of tune', the result can be a not so successful motor performance.

PERCEPTION: MAKING SENSE OF OUR 'SENSES'

Our body senses are the means by which we collect

information on what is happening around us. 'Perception' is the ability to interpret and establish meaning from the information being received. Information comes to us through seeing, hearing, smelling, tasting and feeling (which includes the sensations that we receive through our skin and body movements). The most influential sensory systems and perceptual processes related to movement and motor skills are as follows:

Vision

The ability to see and make sense of what we see is called *visual perception.* Visual perception enables us to judge distances, estimate the speed and velocity of a moving object, as well as the height and angle of the object. Through visual perception your child can determine the appropriate movements to make in order to catch a tennis ball, beach ball or cricket ball.

Visual perception also enables us to sort out foreground from background, and to exclude unnecessary visual interference when trying to attend to one particular task. It is the means by which we recognise and memorise the differences and similarities in shapes, pictures and objects, and it tells us if parts of an object or picture are missing.

Visual perception and memory are important for writing and reading. They define the nature of shapes such as their angle, size, orientation and dimensions so that we can accurately produce them in the correct order or sequence onto paper. It enables your child to successfully complete jigsaws and puzzles, as well as helping him to participate in card games and other activities requiring visual recognition and memory.

Hearing

Listening and making sense of what we hear is called *auditory perception*. If we hear a siren when driving a car, we know that we need to take certain action in response to that sound. When your child hears the school bell ring, it is important that he knows what it means. Auditory perception and remembering what is said, is important for following instructions. Children with an Attention Deficit Disorder and language problems usually have difficulties in this area. It can be hard for them to follow instructions when being taught complex motor skills. When clumsiness and poor coordination are already in the 'package' of problems, it makes it harder to perfect motor skills.

Feeling

We need to know what our bodies are experiencing and doing if we are to move with ease and successfully perfect a motor skill. This information comes via our skin, muscles, tendons and joints.

Tactile perception refers to the information we receive through the sense of touch. It provides us with information on the properties of objects which we manipulate with our hands and fingers. Tactile perception enables children to appreciate the qualities of an object they are handling. For example, is the toy or object soft, hard, rough, smooth, big, little, warm or cold? Through tactile perception, children are able to locate their hankies, lunch money or small toys in their pockets without looking. They are able to locate where they are being touched on their bodies and the nature of the touch. All this information comes through the skin.

Kinaesthesia is a word used to describe the ability to appreciate what our arms, legs and overall body is doing without looking. This sense allows children to position a tennis racket or cricket bat while they keep their eye on the ball. It also tells children the speed of their movements. When children run up or down stairs carrying a large toy or school books and cannot see the steps, it is the sense of kinaesthesia that tells them where to put their feet so that they can ascend or descend safely. This sensory information comes from within muscles, tendons and joints.

WHAT OUR SENSES TEACH US

Body Awareness

Body awareness is important when children participate in and learn new motor skills. It refers to your child's knowledge of different parts of his body and what each part is capable of doing. Body awareness is the understanding of how to use our bodies in the most efficient way to maximise our in-built capabilities. Body awareness can influence your child's drawings of himself and others. In order to draw recognisable figures, your child needs to have developed the knowledge of where body parts such as arms, legs, facial features 'belong'.

Spatial Awareness

Spatial awareness refers to the appreciation of the relationship of objects to each other, and how our own bodies relate to those objects. Your child needs to have developed good spatial awareness in order to successfully participate in team sports such as soccer, netball and basketball. Such sports involve catching, kicking or holding a ball while manoeuvring around team mates and the opposition. Walking and manoeuvring through a crowded room carrying drinks is another example of spatial awarness!

Knowing 'Left' and 'Right'

The word 'laterality' is sometimes used to describe the knowledge within ourselves of left and right. It is knowing which is our right hand without relying on visual clues such as our watch to give us the answer. The knowledge of 'left' and 'right' is important when following directions such as 'turn right', 'move to the left', etc. Lack of well-established hand preference and the inability to know left from right is a common feature amongst children who are uncoordinated in motor skills.

Directionality

'Directionality' is a term used to describe our understanding of the way objects and people are facing. It is the appreciation of left and right on others and the direction of objects and shapes. Your child requires the concept of directionality to know how to write letters such as 'b', 'd', 'p' and 'q'. Directionality is also important in knowing where the top, bottom, and corners of a page are, and to work from left to right when writing words and sentences. As adults, we need to have directionality well-established in order to follow road maps efficiently.

PLANNING AND ORGANISING MOVEMENTS

Planning and organising movements is important in the process of learning and perfecting motor skills. Usually the term 'motor planning' is used to describe this process, and refers to the ability to work out the 'plan of action' before we launch into the motor activity. Motor planning requires organising sensory and perceptual information so that the skill performed comprises smoothly executed movements.

In order to motor plan, we need to draw on past experiences of movements and to organise those experiences into the correct sequence of movements. Complex motor skills such as skiing, riding a bike, playing golf, writing and playing musical instruments require motor planning during the learning process. Once the skill is refined and perfected, less motor planning and organisation is required. This is achieved through practice. Practice provides the opportunity for the series of movements which make up the skill to be 'programed', so that the response becomes automatic with little effort required to successfully perform the task. Think about the degree of motor planning and organisation required when learning how to tie a shoelace. With practice, the finger movements of tying the bows becomes automatic and routine. When this skill is accomplished, children can perform the task very quickly, without having to think or even look at what they are doing. The same also applies to learning the piano or any other musical instrument. Once the correct finger movements have been learnt, they become automatic, so the child is then able to focus on the dynamics and sensitivity of the music.

Motor memory is also important in the planning and organising process. Motor memory enables us to store-up information from previous experiences and to apply them to new and varied situations. We may not have ridden a bike for years but we can still do it despite a time lapse.

MUSCLE TONE AND STRENGTH

Muscle tone relates to the constant underlying state of contraction or tension within our muscles. Even fully relaxed muscles contain a certain degree of tension. If however, there is too much tension within muscle groups, or not enough tension, the quality of movements can be affected. Through sustained muscle tone, we are able to maintain antigravity postures, such as sitting and standing. Muscle strength relates to the ability of the body to exert force, especially against resistance. Muscle tone and strength are important factors in alleviating fatigue and sustaining endurance. When children's muscle tone or strength is not quite as proficient as it should be, moving quickly and with agility is more difficult.

CONTROLLING UNNECESSARY MOVEMENTS

In the process of perfecting a motor skill, a great deal of effort — accompanied by over-exaggerated and unnecessary movements — usually occurs. Just observe people learning to ski, ice-skate, swim or serve a tennis ball. Practice provides opportunity to select and perfect the necessary movements. When this is achieved, the movements are performed with a minimum of effort, look smooth, rhythmical and well-coordinated.

Children learning to perfect motor skills also display unnecessary movements until the skill is perfected, and children who are having difficulties in motor coordination lack the skills or motor maturity necessary to refine those movements. Sometimes the terms 'overflow movements' or 'compensatory movements' are used to describe unnecessary movements or postures in children who seem clumsy and uncoordinated.

BALANCE

Balance is the ability to maintain equilibrium when our body assumes an unstable posture or is placed in an unstable situation. The ability to maintain balance is influenced by other body systems which include vision, touch, kinaesthesia and the balance mechanism within the inner ear. Balance is sometimes described as 'dynamic balance' or 'static balance'.

Dynamic balance refers to the ability to maintain balance while we are moving. For example, roller-skating or walking on top of a brick wall.

Static balance refers to the ability to maintain balance while standing still. For example, standing still on an unstable surface such as a boat, standing on one leg to put on a shoe, or even maintaining balance while doing a handstand!

Both dynamic and static balance are important factors in the development and acquisition of motor skills. If your child is having difficulty with balance, this may make him nervous of swings, walking along balance beams, climbing playground equipment, standing on unstable surfaces and learning to ride a bike. He may need extra encouragement to do these things.

ATTENTION AND CONCENTRATION

To learn any new skill and successfully accomplish it, children first need to be able to exclude extraneous distractions around them and concentrate on the task at hand. It is very difficult (and dangerous!) to teach your child scissor skills if they are more interested in something else happening in the room. 'Attention' is the ability to exclude distractions, while 'concentration' is the ability to focus on the task itself. Daydreaming, being fidgety, easy to distract and impulsive, can be a block to learning and perfecting complex motor skills, and are common problems amongst children who are clumsy and uncoordinated.

MOTIVATION

Motivation is an important aspect to consider when children are confronted with the challenge of learning and refining motor skills. Some children may have an in-built interest and talent in certain activities, and their motivation for perfecting the skill comes from their ongoing success. Other children may be motivated to learn and practise a motor skill because their friends enjoy the activity — if they wish to be part of that circle of friends it is important for them to be reasonably competent in the activity that binds the group. It is very difficult for a child to learn more complex motor skills if they do not have a particular talent in that area, or if there are no external influences to encourage the inner drive to learn and perfect. It is therefore important to praise all attempts your child may make at a task which is obviously difficult for them. Try not to focus on or emphasise the failed attempts.

KEY POINTS

1. Many factors influence your child's ability to perform motor skills in a smooth, coordinated and graceful manner.
2. No one factor works in isolation. All are dependent on each other for ultimate perfection of a motor skill.
3. We need to understand the underlying processes that result in 'fluent and flowing' movements, in order to help children who seem clumsy and uncoordinated.

Many factors influence the ability to be successful in motor skills.

CHAPTER 4

STUMBLES AND FUMBLES: THE DIFFICULTIES

There is great diversity of abilities and difficulties amongst all children. No one child is the same. These abilities and difficulties may appear quite distinct in children who seem clumsy and uncoordinated. Some children may experience problems with writing and fine manipulative movements. Other children may have trouble with their gross motor skills, and yet be quite proficient in writing and fine motor skills. Children with significant motor difficulties may experience problems in all areas. This chapter highlights the most common problem areas and the effects on children.

LEAPING BEFORE LOOKING: PROBLEMS IN CONCENTRATION

Clumsiness can be associated with those children who are hyperactive and impulsive. These children tend to rush at a task and are generally careless because they are easily distracted. They find it hard to sit down and settle into any one particular activity, and so tend to flit from one thing to another. Children who are impulsive often find colouring in neatly between lines difficult and writing can be messy.

They are the ones whose grandma needs to be warned of an impending visit, so precious ornaments can be removed because, easily excited on arrival, these children rush through the house, tripping and knocking things over. In other words, they are the children who seem like the proverbial 'bull in the china shop' and who tend to 'leap before they look'.

Clumsiness and poor coordination can also be associated with children who are daydreamers. They also can easily trip over and knock grandma's ornaments off the shelf because their mind seems elsewhere and, like hyperactive children, they find it hard to focus on what they should be doing. As indicated earlier, such children with in-built concentration difficulties are often diagnosed as having an Attention Deficit Disorder with or without hyperactivity. They frequently have learning problems at school and many of the difficulties detailed in this chapter.

Tripping and bumping into objects can be due to concentration difficulties and hyperactivity.

Children with poor concentration find it hard to settle down if their day is not organised. As parents, you can help your child be less easily distracted and 'on the move' if you plan the day with set activities and little jobs to do around the house. In other words, these children respond to structure and routine. Try to keep instructions clear and simple when you want your child to do something that requires explanation. Concentration difficulties are common amongst children with motor problems. Difficulties in concentration and what you can do to help are further discussed in Appendix I.

GETTING IN A MUDDLE: DIFFICULTIES WITH MOTOR PLANNING AND ORGANISATION

Many children who are clumsy and uncoordinated easily get into a muddle when faced with learning new and complex skills, or when they have to think and do several things at once, especially if under pressure to complete the activity in a set time. I see older children who easily get into a muddle just trying to put their clothes on correctly. They frequently put something on back to front, or when putting on pants end up with both legs in the one hole. They forget where they have put their belongings, and when in unfamiliar situations they easily get lost because they may have poor spatial awareness and sense of direction. At school, they may take longer to find their way around the school corridors and buildings.

They may not only have difficulties in putting clothes on the right way but also managing knife and fork together, learning to swim, skip, ride a bike and any other skilled motor task. Writing is usually very difficult, as not only do these children have to organise their fingers to hold the pencil correctly, but also produce the correct shape of the letter, keep on the line, space the words and translate their thoughts on to paper as well as to listen to the teacher speaking.

These children often have not sorted out which is their dominant hand, so may swap from one hand to the other. They also have difficulty in knowing which is right and left on themselves and others.

Children who easily get in a muddle often have some degree of motor planning difficulty. They find it hard to organise sensory and perceptual information to develop the 'plan of action' that will result in the correct movement. They take longer to remember and organise what they have previously learnt, and find it hard to get started on an activity because they cannot quite sort out which movement comes first. When placed in new or different situations, they may find it hard to adapt learnt skills to changed circumstances. I remember seeing a six-year-old boy who practised and practised at home to perfect a somersault so he could keep up with his class mates in the gym class. His mother reported he could do it at home, but 'froze' under the pressure of performing the skill in the large school gymnasium — in front of his teacher and class mates. He finally attempted the somersault but it fell far short of the standard that he had achieved at home. Such experiences can be very disappointing for children.

Children who are disorganised in this way, may initially look clumsy and uncoordinated. However, once they have learnt and practised the new skill, they can be well-coordinated. The main points to remember with these children are:

a. They have difficulty learning new tasks.
b. They are disorganised especially when trying to do several

Some children find planning and organising the necessary movements difficult.

things at once and when under pressure.

c. They find it hard to adapt learnt skills to new and different situations.

You can help your child by teaching him a new skill one step at a time. Once your child has learnt what to do, practise the activity in a variety of situations or by using different materials. For example, skipping on concrete, grass or rougher ground; throwing and catching a variety of different sized balls; painting; drawing; writing with a variety of pens, pencils and brushes.

POOR FLOW OF MOVEMENT: DIFFICULTIES IN COORDINATION

Some children look awkward and uncoordinated in their *overall body movements*, especially when attempting a variety of gross motor skills such as running, climbing, jumping and hopping. Even the way they walk can lack smoothness of movement and gracefulness. These children seem not to be able to coordinate arms and legs together when attempting a movement requiring speed and rhythm. They tend to trip over their own feet, be nervous of swings, climbing frames and unstable surfaces because their balance is not as good as it should be.

Children with difficulties in overall body coordination may seem a bit 'floppy' in their overall movements, and as a result may walk and run heavily. These are the children who lack a spring in their step. This may be due to what is called low muscle tone or hypotonia, which can also result in poor posture and increased joint mobility. These children do not necessarily have difficulties in organising or knowing what to do. Their weakness lies in the quality of the movements due to poor muscle tone or strength, or other factors such as poor vision or balance.

A variety of outdoor activities including swimming, walking, hiking, horse and bike riding can help improve muscle tone and strength. Paediatric physiotherapists are also able to show you the most appropriate specific exercises to do at your home with your child.

As well as difficulties in overall body movements, children may find tasks involving *eye and hand/foot coordination* difficult. Children need to be able to keep their eyes focused on the target in order to judge distances, gauge speed and respond with well-timed and rhythmical movements. Most sports require eye-hand or eye-foot coordination. For example, hitting a ball with a tennis racquet or cricket bat, bouncing and catching a ball, throwing a ball at a target and kicking a ball.

Poor eye-hand coordination can affect your child's ability to perform finer movements such as stacking blocks, sorting cards, tracing a line with a pencil, colouring in between lines and using tools such as a hammer or a screwdriver. Poor eye-hand coordination can affect the quality of your child's writing. She may know how to write letters and words but the quality of her work may not be to the standard of other children her age.

Poor eye-hand and eye-foot coordination can be improved by practising activities that require repetitive movements. These activities include throwing or kicking balls at a target, throwing quoits onto a peg, hitting a suspended ball with a bat, hammering small nails or tacks into wood, cutting with scissors or colouring-in between lines and shapes.

Children may not only have difficulty with eye-hand coordination but also with *fine manipulative movements*. This may be due to poor muscle tone and strength, along with poorly developed kinaesthetic and tactile awareness in the child's fingers and hands. Activities which involve finer movements include holding small beads while threading, holding and manoeuvring a needle while sewing, lacing, buttoning and unbuttoning, holding and manipulating cutlery, maintaining an appropriate grip on a pencil while writing, and cutting with scissors. You can encourage your child's fine manipulative movements by providing games such as marbles, small toy 'transformers', Lego and finger puppets.

(Remember, it is important to have your child's eyes tested if she is having difficulty with eye-hand and eye-foot coordination, and fine manipulative movements.)

Some children may have difficulty with eye-hand/foot coordination.

GETTING DRESSED AND READY FOR SCHOOL

Motor skills also include those tasks which we do every day as a routine, and without much thought. For example, cleaning our teeth, eating with a knife and fork, toileting, washing, showering and getting dressed. Children who appear clumsy and uncoordinated in motor skills may have difficulties in these everyday tasks. This can cause major difficulties and pressure, especially when getting ready for school and at school itself.

Children who have difficulty with fine manipulative movements may find doing up buttons tricky. Other children who are impulsive, disorganised and easily get into a muddle may also have difficulty locating the correct button hole. They may find it hard to know which way a garment should be put on because they are unable to sort out back from front, left from right, top from bottom. Putting socks on with the heel of the sock correctly orientated and learning to do up shoelaces takes them much longer to accomplish than it does their peers. Learning to do up the school tie for older children is a particular challenge, as it is a skill that requires considerable organisation and planning.

Many children I see are also messy eaters. They may have difficulties chewing and swallowing, as well as coordinating both hands together when attempting to use a knife and fork. They may not be able to hold the cutlery firmly because of a weak grip, or they may exert too much pressure onto the cutlery, sending the vegies everywhere! Many parents find the family meal a stressful experience — especially if their child who is impulsive and easily distracted not only scatters the vegetables but knocks and spills drinks everywhere.

Children with motor difficulties often find cleaning their teeth a challenge. They may squeeze the toothpaste tube too hard and find screwing the cap back onto the tube tricky, as well as the actual manoeuvring of the toothbrush inside the mouth.

Difficulties in toileting can cause major anxiety for school-age children, teachers and parents. If your child has fine motor difficulties, he may find zippers, press studs or buttons difficult to manage, as well as using the toilet paper and wiping himself properly. This may be due to poor body awareness, or poor kinaesthetic perception and motor planning difficulties. His impulsiveness and difficulty with concentration may also add to his problem.

If your child is experiencing significant difficulties with dressing, eating, toileting and other self-care tasks, occupational therapists can guide you to the best ways to help your child overcome these difficulties.

PEN TO PAPER: WRITING DIFFICULTIES

The ability to write quickly and legibly is important for children to be able to keep up with school work. Understandably, writing difficulties cause parents and children much anxiety.

In order to be proficient, fluent and legible in writing, children need to master the movement patterns of letter and word formation so that the process of writing becomes automatic with minimal effort and planning. If this is not achieved, attention is focused on the mechanics of writing, compromising the free-flow of thought and expression.

Writing is a complex motor activity comprising a number of essential components. This includes overall body posture, eye-hand coordination, fine manipulative movements, motor planning, visual, auditory and kinaesthetic perception and language skills. Writing difficulties among clumsy and uncoordinated children are very common and are frequently the main cause of referral to occupational therapy services. Writing is a motor skill which children cannot escape from.

Some children have poor posture at the table with tense

and awkward pencil grips. This makes relaxed and flowing movements difficult. Other children may have perceptual, planning and organisational problems which result in poorly formed letters, reversals, erratic spacing and poor alignment. Others may reverse words or find it hard to write in a straight line, while others may not even know where to begin on the page. Children who are poor readers and spellers find writing difficult because they do not know what letters and sounds make up the words to be written. Their writing problems differ from those children whose difficulties are motor based.

Of all the motor skills with which your child may be experiencing difficulty, writing is often the most subject to criticism and negative comments. This can add to her stress and anxiety, is counter-productive, and does little to help improve the quality of her writing. Children need positive support and encouragement to overcome writing difficulties. It is a learnt motor skill which does not come naturally, as with all skilled motor tasks.

PLAY, BUT NOT MUCH PLEASURE

As we can already see, every aspect of these children's daily lives may be affected. This also includes play skills. Play is a vital part of any child's development. Through play, children not only learn about the world around them but also how to get on with others, learn rules and problem solve. They learn how to express their creativity, discover their talents, make friends and develop confidence. However, clumsy and uncoordinated children may develop poor play skills. Sometimes, I see children whose play is stereotyped (in that they play the same games over and over again), mechanical, lacking experimentation, variability and adventure, all of which require some degree of organisation. One child I remember kept making the same predictable models out of large Lego because he was unable to make his models more varied and interesting due to his planning and organisational difficulties.

Sometimes these children seem destructive with toys. This is often not intentional destructiveness but rather associated with an inability to play with the toy in an organised and coordinated manner. Children with motor difficulties can often be rough with their toys because they lack the necessary skills to handle them appropriately.

These children are often the ones with whom others will not play because they are unable to keep up in games and are 'not much fun to play with'. Participation demands extra effort and perseverance. Sometimes it is easier to give up, stay indoors and watch television rather than be teased and rejected. As a result, these children are frequently accused of laziness.

Children with motor difficulties may become particularly assertive when playing with others. They may do this so that the games and rules are played on their terms and in such a way that they can handle the situation and not present as a failure to the group. This often leads to fights.

If play skills are affected, children are at risk of becoming socially isolated from their peers. They fail to develop friendships and as a result, lose confidence in themselves and become unhappy and lonely children. This is a sad situation for both the child and family.

As parents you can help your child's play skills by playing a variety of fun games with him, both indoors and outdoors. Invite one or two other children to your home to foster friendships. Try and play with the children, so you can supervise and guide their games and interactions with each other. These games can include old favourites such as chasings, hide and seek, treasure hunts, Simon Says and I Spy.

Children with motor difficulties are at risk of becoming socially isolated.

KEY POINTS

1. Children with difficulties in motor skills are often hyperactive, impulsive or daydreamers. This affects their ability to concentrate and can be a major problem when trying to learn and perfect a motor skill.
2. Children with difficulties in motor skills may have problems in perceptual, motor planning and organisational skills. They easily get into a muddle, especially when placed under pressure. They look clumsy and uncoordinated when learning new tasks or when forced to perform familiar tasks under pressure or out of routine.
3. Poor overall body coordination, eye and hand coordination and fine manipulative movements may be due to any of the above factors, as well as poor vision, balance and muscle tone.
4. Difficulties in motor skills can affect writing, everyday self-care tasks and play skills.
5. Children with motor difficulties may lose confidence in themselves and are at risk of becoming socially isolated from their peers.

CHAPTER 5

COPING CONFIDENTLY: FOCUSING ON SELF-ESTEEM

Children with motor difficulties are vulnerable. They can easily lose confidence in themselves, due to the difficulties in attaining a level of physical competence which seems to come so easily to others. It is upsetting for all of us to see our children always coming last in running races or never being picked to go on a team. We know that for most children this experience hurts, especially if it is a common occurrence — reflecting an ongoing problem in motor coordination. Yet these experiences are only some of many which daily face clumsy and uncoordinated children. For these children, the sense of failure can be so overwhelming, that confidence is lost in most of the activities they undertake. This can have serious repercussions in the long-term, if a pattern of sensing failure and then feeling a lack of confidence is established.

In this chapter we look at the issues of self-esteem, and ways of helping children overcome negative feelings associated with poor self-esteem. This is the essential ingredient for helping children with motor difficulties. These children's difficulties do not readily go away, so building up confidence and self-esteem is important. If we can help children recognise their strengths and reinforce them while they are young, negative experiences and their undesirable consequences can be overridden.

SELF-ESTEEM: WHAT IS IT?

'Self-esteem' refers to how we feel about ourselves and how we perceive what others think of us. 'Self-worth' is another way of describing these feelings. If we feel great about ourselves and our achievements, the inner drive to meet challenges and succeed is reinforced. We need to like ourselves and feel we are of value to ourselves and others. 'High self-esteem' describes this positive belief in our abilities and achievements. On the other hand, if we regard ourselves as 'hopeless', 'not very clever' or 'useless', this reflects a poor image of ourselves which can affect our approach to those we meet and the way we handle daily events. We can lose motivation, interest and a zest for life because we have come to think of ourselves as not much good at anything. Such feelings can negate all that is positive and potentially fruitful in our lives.

Throughout life most of us encounter periods of 'high self-esteem' and 'low self-esteem'. If we mainly experience low self-esteem, it is much more difficult to overcome negative feelings because we have come to believe that success is not possible.

Children 'tune in' to the attitudes of those around them. If they are constantly faced with negative comments and attitudes, they will absorb the negative messages and believe that is how things are. If these negative messages are continuously directed towards them, it is very hard to undo the image they may have developed of themselves once it is ingrained. When they do achieve and experience success, no joy is felt because they have learnt to believe that life is a failure. It is important for a parent to step in before this cycle is established in their child.

'LOOK AT ME!': EXPERIENCING SUCCESS

Children with motor difficulties need to experience success if they are to receive the positive messages within themselves and from others. So often I see children for occupational therapy who, when presented with an activity, respond with comments such as 'I can't', 'I'm tired' or 'It's too hard'. Sometimes they do not have to say anything; their difficult behaviour gives me the message. When this occurs, I know that what I am expecting of the child is either beyond his capabilities or he fears failure. To handle such situations, children often develop set strategies to avoid a potentially threatening situation. It is therefore important to adjust the game or activity to an easier level so they are successful. It may mean playing bat and ball games with a softer or larger ball, moving the target closer or discreetly losing at card or any other games.

I remember a seven-year-old girl who had considerable motor difficulties affecting all aspects of her school and home life. She had picked up such negative feelings about herself, that her behaviour was extremely non-compliant when remedial activities for her difficulties were attempted. Her behaviour changed for the better when games and activities were presented at a level at which she knew she could succeed. This initially meant giving her games and activities at the preschool level. Once she knew that she was in a situation where failure did not occur, it was then possible to give her more challenging and age-appropriate tasks.

As parents we need to remember that our children may well be facing stressful and demoralising situations at school, especially in the playground where life can be tough for children with motor difficulties. We have no control of these situations. However, at home we do have control. Home should be a 'safe haven' for children to experience feelings of being valued, loved and secure. It is very difficult for children to pick up these positive messages if their attempts at motor skills are treated with negative criticism or lack of interest. Adjusting activities so children experience success is not a question of 'giving in', but rather consciously providing an atmosphere which helps restore shattered confidence. Confidence restored and nurtured helps children face the unhappy feelings that come from being teased and placed on the outer by peers. Children do not have enough life-experiences to see unpleasant incidents in perspective; what seems to be a trivial incident to an adult can in the eyes of a child be a major catastrophe.

Children are very blunt when it comes to telling others of their weaknesses. Building up confidence at home by helping children feel like 'winners' and good about themselves can help override the 'knocks' that may come their way during the day.

ESTABLISHING REALISTIC EXPECTATIONS

High self-esteem can be fostered in a number of ways. The following are some comments and suggestions which may help you with your child.

- When teaching skilled motor tasks to children, a common mistake is to have too high an expectation of the level of perfection a child should attain. For example, we may have in our minds an image of a superstar tennis player, and so when teaching children how to handle a tennis racquet somehow we expect them also to be superstar tennis players.

For those children who already have difficulties achieving age-appropriate motor skills, trying to perfect complex motor skills to a level far beyond their competence is not only unrealistic but adds stress and promotes a high level of frustration.

Children need to be able to develop motor skills at their own pace under gentle and encouraging guidance. I'm sure all of us have come across situations where parents overload their children with too many instructions which are far from encouraging. A constant barrage of comments, such as 'keep your eye on the ball!', 'throw the ball up straight!', 'follow through!', 'don't just stand there!', 'don't drop the racquet head!', 'try harder!', 'not that way', will hardly endear the child to tennis. If children are bombarded with a multitude of instructions and negative feedback on their attempts, they are highly unlikely to want to take up that activity as an interest or hobby.

• When teaching motor skills, focus on one aspect at a time. This, backed up by encouraging feedback, is more likely to achieve greater gains in the long-run. Comments like 'well done!', 'that's better!', 'try it this way!' 'wow, that's great' are far more likely to get your child on side, keen and motivated to pursue and perfect a skill. This will lead on to a sense of achievement and positive feeling, rather than being overwhelmed, pressured and frustrated. We need to be especially aware of this when encouraging sporting activities and interests with children who are clumsy and uncoordinated. As adults we need to keep reminding ourselves:

— are the skills being taught age-appropriate?

— is my child ready to attempt that level of motor competence?

— am I giving encouraging feedback?

• For those of us who were good at school sports, it can be particularly frustrating if we have a child who is not well-coordinated. We want our children to benefit from the praise, social standing and personal satisfaction that we most likely experienced in our youth. Physical fitness and being 'sporty' are still held in high regard, so it can be disappointing if our children seem to miss out on all the benefits that come from excelling in sports. However, we need to remind ourselves that there is more to life than being brilliant on the footy field or squash court. What counts, is that our children grow up being happy and feeling valued, with a purpose in life and, above all, that they grow up with friends and a supportive family.

RECOGNISING THE DIFFICULTIES

The first step towards helping children with poor motor development is to recognise and to have insight into their difficulties. Often the problems can be overlooked because they may be subtle, especially those related to motor planning and organisation. The fact that your child can seem coordinated one day but not the next, when situations and circumstances change, can be quite confusing. Being tuned into your child's variability of motor performance is important.

The suggested activities in this book cover a wide range of skills that clumsy and uncoordinated children often have difficulty with. By selecting those activities which you think address your child's specific area of weakness, you can help his motor skill development. For example, your child may not be particularly good at fine manipulative movements, eye-hand coordination or doing several things at once such as catching a ball while running. Choose therefore those sections which you think may help your child.

Specific games and activities can be encouraged so that your child has the opportunity to improve at them and thus gain confidence. It may be difficult, however, for you to identify the specific areas of weakness. This is why you may find it helpful to be in touch with therapy services, so that the most appropriate activities are focused upon.

The main thing to remember is that your child needs his confidence boosted. The aim of encouraging specific activities is to provide opportunity for him to practise the things that he finds too hard, in a caring and supportive environment where there is no pressure to achieve a certain standard in a set time. Your child needs the opportunity to practise the skills at his own pace. To boost his confidence and overcome his feelings of failure, the activities should be fun and carried out when everyone has the time and is feeling relaxed.

Many parents I meet often say they feel guilty if they do not set time aside daily to work with their child. Remember children need to receive positive messages. Feelings of guilt only add to inner tension, and children easily sense and absorb negative feelings that parents are experiencing. It is the quality of the time that you spend with your child that is important, not the quantity.

Praise should be given at any attempts your child makes at a motor skill which is obviously difficult for them. They need these boosts to keep practising and achieving. The aim is not to wait till the 'perfect result' is achieved before credit is given but rather to encourage whatever attempts are made, as these children are prone to give up easily.

ENCOURAGING STRENGTHS

Every child is good at something. It is important to recognise children's strengths and encourage their development. It is easy to focus on a child's weaknesses and lose sight of, or overlook, potential talents and interests. Through interests we meet others with similar interests and so friendships develop. If your child appears to be linking up with another child, encourage that child to come to your home so the common interests can be fostered. Suggest also that they come on family outings and picnics so that the children experience the same events and 'happenings' together.

Activities may need to be adjusted so children can experience success.

Some children may be interested in collecting certain toys to make up a series, while others may gravitate towards computer games. Other children may have a vivid imagination and enjoy making up stories which can be recorded or written down. Keep your eyes open to the games and activities that your child tends to naturally gravitate towards, and see if there are ways that these interests can be developed and channelled in a positive way. Remember, the aim is to foster positive self-esteem by giving your child the message that he is good at something and that he does have his own special gifts and talents. If you are stuck for ideas, Chapter 7 discusses some appropriate leisure activities to consider for uncoordinated and non-'sporty' children.

KEY POINTS

1. Clumsy and uncoordinated children are at risk of developing poor self-esteem because they find it difficult to keep up with others in sport and physical activities.
2. Children can develop poor self-esteem due to the negative comments and attitudes of others, and by being rejected by their peers or constantly overlooked when participating in sporting activities.
3. To boost children's self-esteem, be positive and encouraging.
4. Allow children to practise at their own pace and at their level of competency those things which they find difficult. Praise and encourage their efforts no matter how far from the 'perfect result' those efforts may be.
5. It is important to foster children's interests and talents and not to always focus on their difficulties.

CHAPTER 6

HELPING AT HOME: SUGGESTED ACTIVITIES

The activities outlined in this chapter are general ideas which you may like to do at home. These activities provide children who are clumsy and uncoordinated with the opportunity to practise and improve those areas of difficulty which they frequently experience. They are activities which can be carried out at home with minimal expense, and can be easily incorporated into family activities. In no way are they meant to be set exercises, to be diligently carried out on a daily basis despite an unwilling child and a busy and stressed parent. If they become 'chores', little will be achieved and all your efforts probably will be counterproductive. The following suggested activities are suitable for children ages five to eleven. You may need to think of how you can make some of them harder or easier according to your child's level of success when trying them. Remember, children respond to games which allow them to experience success and are *fun!* (see Appendix II).

The suggested activities are listed under the following headings:

A. To encourage perceptual skills (looking, listening, feeling)
B. To build up strength
C. To encourage balance and confidence in movement
D. To increase body awareness
E. To help eye-hand and eye-foot coordination

F. To help fine manipulation
G. To encourage motor planning
H. To help writing skills
I. To encourage independence in self-care.

A. TO ENCOURAGE PERCEPTUAL SKILLS

Looking Games

It is important for children to understand what they see. This is called visual perception. If your child is having difficulty with her visual perception, she may find puzzles and jigsaws hard to do. She may also have difficulty working out how constructional toys fit together, especially when trying to follow pictorial instructions. The following games will encourage the development of her visual perceptual abilities.

- **Dominoes:** can be bought from most toy shops. This game involves matching dots or pictures, as well as accurately placing the dominoes. Another fun game to play with dominoes is standing them up in a row on their ends and pushing the end one over so a chain reaction occurs as they fall.
- **Picture and number lotto:** these are also commercially available and involve matching pictures or numbers.
- **Puzzles/jigsaws:** you can make up your own by pasting a picture onto cardboard and then cutting it up into pieces. If you buy commercially made jigsaws, do not buy the ones with too many pieces unless you know your child is capable of doing it with minimal frustration.
- **Mazes:** a pencil and paper game which can be bought in toy shops or educational bookshops. If your child is unable to work out the solution by just looking, use a finger to first work out where the line should be drawn.

- **Sorting:** encourage your child to undertake sorting jobs around the house. For example, sorting screws, nails, buttons, cutlery and even sorting socks that come out of the laundry basket.
- **Matching lids to jars:** collect various size lids and jars. Mix the lids around on the table and see if your child can point to the jar which fits the lid.
- **Card games:** involve visual discrimination and the ability to recognise differences and similarities between shapes. The ability to do this is important for reading and writing.
- **Memory:** place mixed paired picture cards on the table face down in a row. Start off with only four or five pairs. Turn two cards over at a time to see if they are a pair. If not, the other player has a turn. Gradually increase the number of pairs on the table. Use children's picture cards for younger children and standard playing cards for older children.
- **Snap:** this game requires quick recognition of pictures or numbers. Each player has the same number of cards and takes turns to place them face upwards on the table. If the cards are a pair the first player to put their hand on the pile of cards and call 'snap' wins the cards.
- **Memory game:** place three to five objects on the table, for example, a spoon, fork, cup and pencil. Allow your child five seconds to look at all the objects. Then hide the objects under a cloth and remove one. See if your child can tell you which one is missing. It can be made more difficult by increasing the number of objects removed.
- **Pattern copying:** buy a packet of adhesive dots or stars. Stick them on a piece of paper in the corners and middle of the page. See if your child can copy the same design on her piece of paper.

If you have the game 'Connect 4' which is played like noughts and crosses, the tokens in that game can also be used for copying patterns.

• **Block designs:** use approximately ten children's building blocks to make up models such as 'steps', 'bridges' and 'aeroplanes'. See if your child can copy the same model with her blocks. Make it harder by not letting her see you make your model.

• **Sequencing games:** draw a line on a piece of paper and stick the adhesive dots along the line. Draw another line underneath your line and see if your child can copy the same sequence working in an orderly manner from left to right.

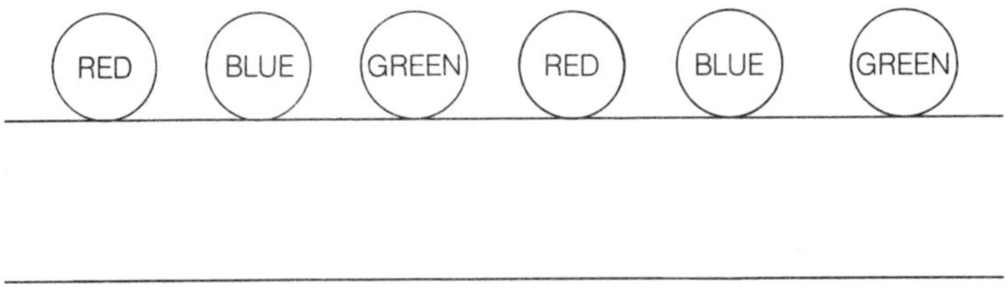

Build a tower out of large Lego (Duplo), using different colours. See if your child can copy your tower exactly.

Thread coloured beads onto a string and encourage your child to copy the same pattern on her string.

• **Torch game:** sit in a slightly darkened room and take turns to locate objects of different shape or colour by shining the torch on the object. For example, finding all the objects that are round, square, rectangular, made out of wood, plastic, hard or soft that are in the room. You need not use a torch but it does make it more fun and helps children focus on the specific shapes and objects in the room.

Listening Games

The following activities encourage auditory perception. They will help your child to practise both attending to and focusing selectively on what she hears. If your child has difficulty in this area, it is important to have her hearing tested by an audiologist. Difficulties in auditory perception can be tested and helped by speech pathologists. The ability to listen and understand what is being said is important for learning and following instructions when being taught complex motor skills.

- **Tap out simple rhythms:** either by clapping your hands together or tapping your hand on the table. Commence with simple rhythms and see if your child can reproduce the sound you make. The game should be played without your child watching your hands.
- **Bouncing ball:** stand behind your child and bounce a ball. See if she can tell you how many times you bounced the ball. Start off with a small number of bounces, and gradually increase the number as your child becomes accurate in her response.
- **Give your child instructions to follow:** you can make these games fun by taking turns to give the instructions. Start off with a simple instruction, as some children cannot manage more than one or two instructions at a time. Increase the number of components within the instruction as your child succeeds. For example:

i) clap hands, turn around and then jump up and down!

ii) draw a blue circle at the top of your page, red square in the middle of your page.

iii) *Bring me:*
start with objects in the same room such as a newspaper,

biro and cushion. Gradually increase the number of items and include objects out of other rooms.

- **Listening to different sounds:** make different sounds with everyday objects, such as teaspoon tapping a cup, clicking your fingers, tapping the table with a pencil, stamping your feet. Let your child see how the sounds are made then encourage her to close her eyes or turn around. Repeat the sounds in different order and see if your child can tell you what the sound was and in what order they came. Remember, keep the number of components to one or two and gradually increase them as your child succeeds.
- **Filling in missing words:** say together words of a familiar nursery rhyme or song that your child knows well. Repeat the song but miss out one word and see if your child can tell you the missing word. Increase the difficulty by leaving more words out. For example, 'Little Peter rabbit had a fly upon his nose' then repeat 'Little Peter ... had a ... upon his nose'. Let your child fill in the missing words.
- **Remove distractions:** when playing the above games, make sure you have turned the television or radio off because this will make it very difficult for your child to concentrate on your instructions. Also, make sure your child is looking at you when you are giving the instructions.

'Feeling' Games

'Feeling' games enable children to successfully undertake motor skills without always needing to look at what they are actually doing. For example, a child needs to be able to feel what her fingers are doing when she is playing the piano, so that she can read the music at the same time. Understanding what we feel and knowing what our fingers, arms and legs are doing without looking is called tactile and kinaesthetic perception. The following games encourage these perceptual skills.

- **Finding hidden objects:** place everyday objects such as a spoon, money and fork into a cloth bag or school back pack. See if your child can find the objects by feeling only.
- **Where did I touch you?:** stand behind your child or encourage her to close her eyes. Touch her quickly and lightly with your finger tips. See if she can tell you where she has been touched. Make the game fun by taking turns.
- **Moving arms and fingers:** this game is played with eyes closed. Hold lightly onto your child's arm or one of her fingers and slowly move it up or down once. Ask your child which direction her arm or finger moved. An alternative to this game is to move your child's arm, hand or finger and see if she can follow the same movement with the other limb.
- **Pin the tail on the donkey:** draw a donkey minus its tail or a car minus a wheel. Your child looks at the incomplete picture either on the table or pinned up on the wall. With her eyes closed, she must try to pin the missing part accurately on the picture.
- **Drawing on back:** sit on the floor with your child's back to you. Trace shapes such as a circle, square or letters and see if your child can tell you what shape it is. Alternatively, see if your child can reproduce the shape on the floor with a finger. Between each drawing 'rub out' the previous one. Take turns.

B. TO BUILD UP STRENGTH

The pursuit of leisure activities such as swimming, archery, bushwalking and horseriding can help your child's overall strength and endurance so that he can keep up with others in physically active games. The following ideas are aimed mainly at building up shoulder girdle, upper-arm and grip strength.

- **Wheelbarrows:** hold your child at the knees, rather than at the ankles. You can make it fun by encouraging your child to carry something on his back, and go around a simple obstacle course such as around the dining-room table or coffee table and over a cushion. If this is a strain on your back, you should give it a miss.

- **Arm wrestles:** sit opposite your child with elbows on the table. Hold each other's hand and encourage your child to push against the resistance. Obviously you will be stronger, so let your child win to make it enjoyable.
- **Tug of war:** twist a bathroom towel to make a 'rope'. Play

'tug-of-war' with your child, either standing or sitting on the floor.

- **Crunching newspaper:** crunch up sheets of newspaper into a ball. Once a few balls have been made see if your child can throw them at a target.
- **Swinging from overhead ladder:** usually set up in local parks and children's playgrounds. You will need to support your child until he has enough strength and confidence to swing from rung to rung independently.

- **Pottery clay, firm Playdough, plasticine:** provide the opportunity to strengthen your child's hands and finger muscles by rolling, squeezing, pinching and pounding.
- **Squeezing a thick sponge:** in one hand or both hands also helps strengthen grip. This can be done while in the bath.
- **Water games:** are commercially available toys and involve working the fingers against resistance. Watering the

household potplants with a squeeze spray bottle also provides an opportunity to build up strength in the hands.

- **Pushing a horizontal broom handle against resistance:** your child tries to push you up to one end of the room or across a line on the floor. Make sure the elbows are kept slightly bent rather than stiffening them at the elbow joint.

C. TO ENCOURAGE BALANCE AND CONFIDENCE IN MOVEMENT

Encouraging your child to experience a variety of movement sensations will help improve her balance and build up her confidence when standing and walking on unstable surfaces.

- **Playground equipment:** including swings, slippery dips, balance beams, climbing ladders — all of which are set up in children's playgrounds.

• **Trampoline:** or exercise rebounder if available. It is important to supervise your child, especially on a trampoline. If she is nervous, start off just sitting and bouncing, then kneeling and finally standing. Once your child has gained confidence, she can try:
— jumping and clapping her hands in front of her body, behind her back, above her head
— jumping with her feet apart and then together
— hopping on one foot, then changing to the other foot
— jumping with one foot in front of the other, then feet together, and then with one leg in front of the other
— jumping sideways, backwards and forwards
— catching a ball and counting while doing any of the above

- **Rolling:** down a grassy slope.
- **Hopscotch:** if your child finds it hard to hop, try jumping with both feet in each square first.
- **Walking along a two to three metre taped line:** place the tape on the floor. Encourage your child to walk heel to toe along the line, forwards and then backwards. Take turns and keep a score on how many times the line was stepped off. Make it fun by having prizes.
- **Walking on stilts:** these can be made easily out of tins and rope.

- **Stepping stones:** place cardboard cut-out shapes of circles, squares, triangles on the floor. See if your child can follow the course by placing one foot on each 'stone'. Vary the distance between each 'stone'.

- **Balance in crawl position:** let your child practise keeping balance by lifting up one leg or one arm. Make it more difficult by asking her to lift up an arm and a leg at the same time.

- **Balance board:** if there is a carpenter in the house, the balance board can be made up in the following dimensions. It is best to place it on carpet so it will not slip and also cover it with carpet.

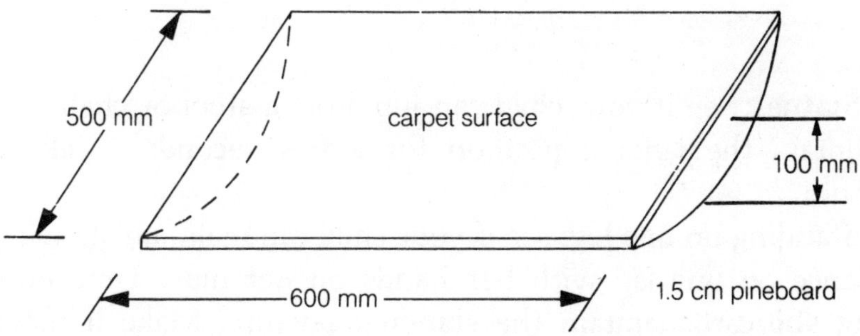

• **Balance board activities:** have your child balance while kneeling upright or standing. Let her try throwing and catching a ball while keeping balance or walking around the edge of the board.

• **Statues:** see if your child can jump off a stool or chair and maintain the landing position for a few seconds — like a 'statue'.

• **Standing on one leg:** see if your child can maintain standing balance on one leg with her hands on her hips. Time how long she can maintain the standing posture. Make it more difficult by asking her to swing her free leg.

D. TO INCREASE BODY AWARENESS

The following games will help your child to be aware of different parts of his body. This is important in establishing the concept of left and right, as well as learning what different parts of the body are capable of doing.

• **Simon Says:** play this game with eyes open or closed. If your child has difficulty following the verbal directions demonstrate the action:

— touch right hand to left shoulder
— touch left hand to right ear
— touch toes, elbows, eye-brows etc
— hands on hips, knees, ankles etc
— bending forwards, sideways, backwards at the waist
— swinging arms

• **Hokey Pokey:** as you go through the song use the words 'right' and 'left' to help reinforce right and left discrimination.

• **Rubbing:** after a shower or bath, encourage your child to dry themselves firmly and briskly to increase body awareness and reinforce right and left.

• **Where can you bend?:** discover all the body parts that can 'bend'. Go through small finger movements and large body movements. For example, bending at the waist, bending the last joint of the little finger.

• **Mirror Game:** stand facing a mirror. Encourage your child to copy movements that you make by looking in the mirror only. For example, waving with the right hand, touching body parts, hand and finger movements.

• **Drawing around your child's body:** when lying on the floor on a large piece of paper. As you draw around your child's body, ask him where you are up to. Once the drawing is complete, let your child draw in his facial features and clothing.

E. TO HELP EYE-HAND AND EYE-FOOT COORDINATION

The following games consist of repetitive movements which will help your child develop a sense of rhythm, timing and judgement of distances. With practice, your child should become more proficient at games requiring eye-hand and eye-foot coordination.

• **Scoop-ball:** this game is commercially available or you can make up your own scoops from empty plastic cordial bottles. There are two types:

i) thread a tennis ball or rubber/foam ball attached to a string through the lid. The aim is to swing the scoop and try and catch the ball in the container.

ii) Cut out the bottom of the bottle into a scoop shape as shown in the diagram below. This game is played with a partner and involves throwing and catching the ball in the scoop.

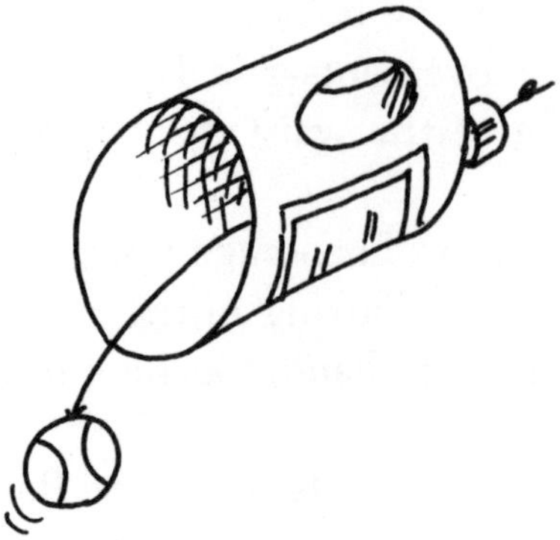

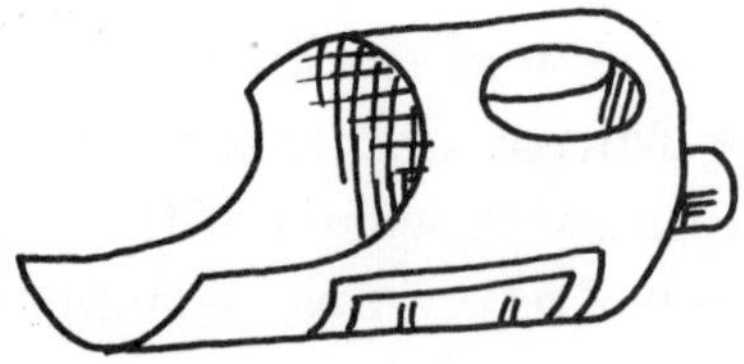

• **Grip ball:** a commercially made game where the bat and ball are made out of velcro so that the ball sticks to the bat.
• **Skittles:** plastic skittle sets can be purchased from toy shops. The game involves rolling a ball along the floor to knock the skittles over.
• **Quoits:** start the game by placing the peg very close to your child. Gradually make it more difficult by increasing the distance.
• **Pouring water from one jug to another:** mark a line on the jug and see if your child can fill only to that line. Hold the jugs up high and away from the body. Make it more interesting by colouring the water.
• **Jump the rope:** attach a light weight to the end of the rope to make the rope whirl faster.

• **Thowing balls:** or even rolled up socks into a basket or bucket. Gradually decrease the size of the container or increase the distance to make the game more challenging.
• **Hitting a suspended ball:** with a bat or racquet. The ball can be placed in a string bag so it can be suspended. Balloons can also be used.
• **Hitting a ball with a rolling pin:** a rolling pin with handles is held in both hands. See if your child can hit a beachball thrown or bounced to them.
• **Kicking ball:** into a large carton. Make it more difficult by placing the box further away.
• **Kicking a beach ball:** with your child lying on the floor, stand in front of her and see if she can kick the ball with both feet together, keeping knees and hips bent.

F. TO HELP FINE MANIPULATION

The following activities encourage a variety of finger movements. It is important for your child to be proficient in fine manipulative movements so he can do up buttons, fastenings, and undertake craft activities at school.

- **Pegging spring-loaded pegs:** using index finger and thumb to open the peg. Pegs can be sorted into colours and placed around the edge of an icecream container to make a 'hat' or 'birthday cake'.
- **Fiddle sticks/pick up sticks:** can be purchased from most toy shops and is a game that can involve the whole family.
- **Tiddly Winks/marbles:** also commercially available games which involve fine manipulative movements.
- **Chinese Checkers/pocket solitaire games:** both games involve picking up pieces with index finger and thumb.
- **Using tweezers:** to pick up threads, pins, buttons, seeds and placing them into a bottle.
- **Pipecleaners:** making shapes and figures by twisting the pipecleaners around each other. Pipecleaners can be purchased from most newsagents.
- **Sewing/lacing cards:** are made out of plastic or cardboard, and can be found in most toy departments. Also, you can make up your own by using large hole tapestry fabric and drawing a simple picture on it which your child has chosen. See if he can sew around the outline of the picture with wool or thick cotton.
- **Scissors:** if your child is having difficulty with scissors, commence with snipping a thin strip of plasticine or cardboard. Make it more difficult by using thinner cardboard, then paper. Practise cutting along straight lines, curving lines, then shapes.
- **Cats Cradle:** a string game which involves making designs with string and encourages isolated finger movements. More suitable for older children. There are books available on various string designs but most tend to be rather complex,

so keep to the simple designs you may know.

- **Threading beads:** threading small beads or coloured macaroni onto a string.

G. TO ENCOURAGE MOTOR PLANNING

The learning of any new or unfamiliar motor skill requires motor planning, especially when one has to do several things at once. The following activities are games which involve several components and require a certain degree of organisation to perfect.

- **Walking around chairs:** position two chairs about two to three metres apart. See if you and your child can walk around the chairs while hitting a balloon to keep it up in the air.
- **Running and weaving between objects:** place boxes about one to two metres apart and encourage running and weaving in between the boxes without knocking into them.

- **Ladder walk:** place a ladder on the ground and see if your child can walk between the rungs forwards, backwards and sideways. See if she can then do it while she is carrying something, for example a beachball, box or large toy.

- **Walking along a line:** make a straight line on the floor out of approximately six metres of masking tape. The game is played by walking along the line without stepping off. As with 'ladder walk' the aim is also to walk forwards, sideways and backwards. See if your child can catch a ball at the same time.
- **Skipping:** is often difficult for clumsy and poorly coordinated children because it involves organising the correct sequence of movements. To teach skipping, as with all skilled motor tasks, teach each stage of the skill separately. This means analysing the components, that is, step first, then hop, step with other leg, then hop. If your child is unable to hop, practise hopping first on an old mattress or exercise rebounder to develop the 'spring'.
- **Rolling game:** involves rolling along the floor towards a goal such as a chair or bucket. Make it more challenging by encouraging your child to hold something in her hands as she rolls, for example an orange. As she rolls, encourage her to put her hands above her head.
- **Motor boats:** involves lying on a carpeted floor on the back with knees bent. It is a game where children pretend to be a boat and 'propel' themselves with their feet and can be played in the hallway. A piece of furniture can be the 'wharf' to manoeuvre towards.
- **Paper folding games:** such as making aeroplanes or a hat. Paper folding books can be purchased from toy shops.
- **Paper weaving:** weaving strips of paper in and out of a slitted sheet of paper to make a place mat.
- **Miming:** a game to be played with the whole family. Take

turns to carry out an action and see if the rest of the family can guess what it is. For example, hammering a nail, putting on a sock, squeezing toothpaste and cleaning teeth.

- **Following a map:** draw a map of the house with 'treasures' placed in various rooms. See if your child can follow the map to find the 'treasures'.
- **Twister:** this game is commercially available. It involves knowing right from left, planning where to place arms and legs as well as keeping balance. It is a fun game which also can involve the whole family.

H. TO HELP WRITING SKILLS

Writing is a complex activity involving coordination, motor planning, fine manipulation, visual and auditory perception and language skills. Children's abilities in these areas vary enormously. Because of its complexity and the variation of abilities and difficulties in children's writing performance, the following ideas are very general. They do, however, cover some of the motor aspects of writing with which clumsy and uncoordinated children frequently have difficulty.

- **Always check your child's posture at the table:**
— feet should be flat on the ground
— desk or table height should not be too high or too low; this may result in a stooped posture or hunched shoulders
— forearms should rest comfortably on the table
— the paper may be tilted slightly to the left for right-handers and slightly to the right for left-handers.
- **Check pencil grip:** if the pencil grip looks awkward or there is too much tension in the fingers resulting in discomfort and fatigue, try using thicker shaft pencils or a pencil grip. The triangular pencil grips can be purchased from newsagents or alternatively, foam can be wrapped around the pencil.
- **Pencil control activities:**
— tracing around templates of animals or shapes. These can be purchased in toy shops
— playing 'boxes' by varying the distances between the dots to be joined
— dot-to-dot games are commercially available or you can make up your own

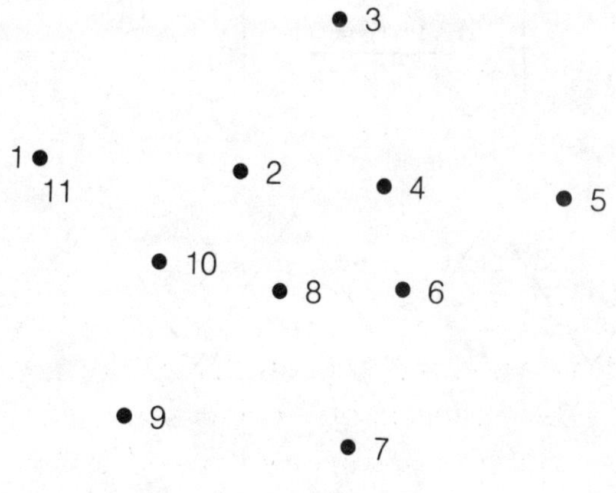

• **To encourage smooth movements:** some children are jerky in their writing movements. On a large piece of paper, encourage your child to trace over the following designs using either a thick paint brush, textas, crayons or pencils. See if he can trace without stopping, going backwards or off the line.

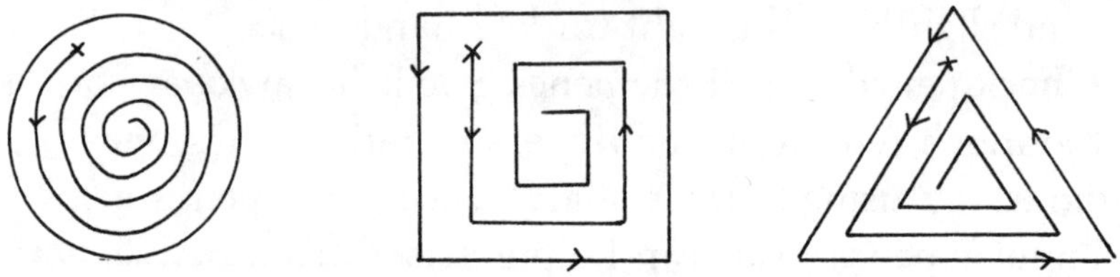

• **To encourage rhythm and speed of movement:** set a slow beat on a metronome or tap the beat yourself and go through the following patterns keeping in time to the beat. Once accuracy has been achieved increase the speed.

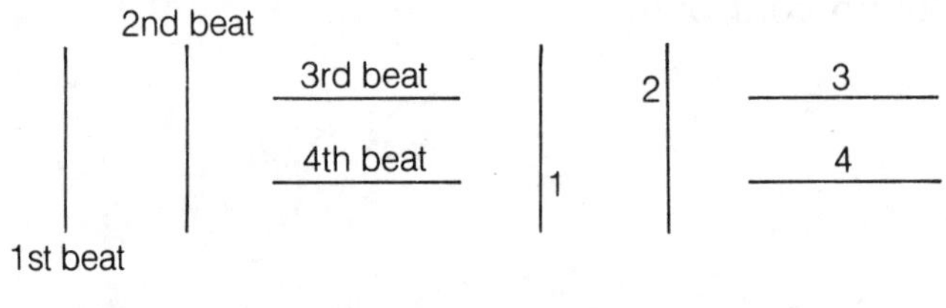

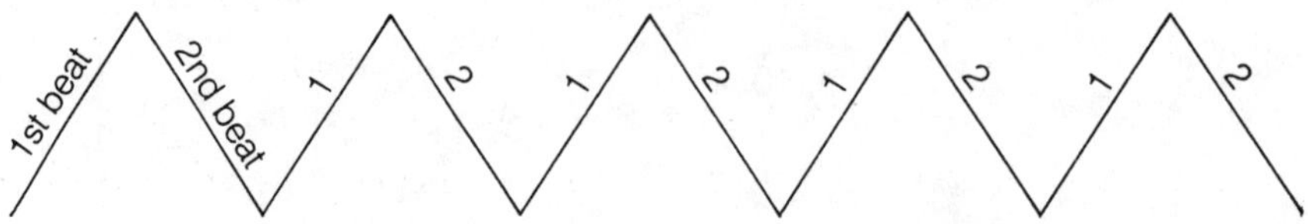

• **To encourage fine pencil control:** the following scribble patterns are ideas to encourage control of the pencil with isolated index and thumb movements. Other scribble patterns include circular movements in either direction and a row of loops. Sometimes it is easier to use a softer lead pencil.

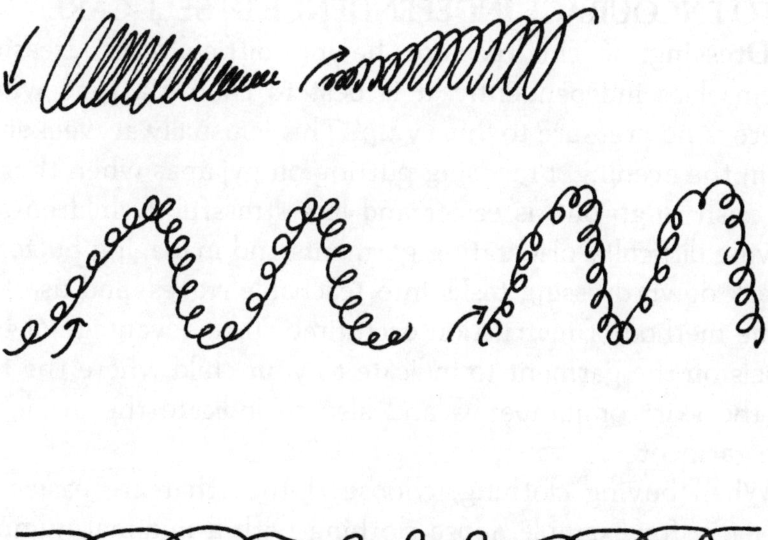

• **To control pencil pressure:** place several sheets of carbon paper and plain paper underneath the writing paper. See if your child can either press firmly to see if the writing is seen through the several layers or to press very lightly so that no impression is made.

• **Practise actual letters:** encourage your child to first practise writing a row of individual letters in the style that is taught at school. Then see if your child can cluster two or three letters together. Keep a check on posture, pencil grip, smoothness of movement, pencil pressure and rhythm. Remember however not to overload your child with too many instructions — just focus on one aspect at a time.

I. TO ENCOURAGE INDEPENDENCE IN SELF-CARE

- **Dressing:** if children are having difficulty in dressing themselves independently, it is best to choose a time when there is no pressure to 'hurry up'. This is usually at weekends or in the evening. Practising putting on pyjamas when there's no rush to go out, is easier and less stressful if children are having difficulty orientating garments and managing buttons. Break down dressing tasks into teachable stages, and use the same method of instruction each time. Take advantage of the labels on the garment to indicate to your child where the top of the skirt or jumper is and also to indicate the inside of the garment.

When buying clothing, choose clothes that are easier to manage; for example, loose clothing with a minimal number of buttons and fastenings. Choosing a jumper or T-shirt with a distinctive pattern on the back or front can help orientation.

If your child is having particular difficulty with buttons, practise the fine manipulative movements on a garment away from the body so your child can see clearly which movements are necessary. When practising with buttons on a shirt itself, help your child with all the buttons except the last one. See if she can do this without any assistance. Once this is achieved leave the last two buttons to be completed independently and so on till all buttons on a shirt can be done up without your help. If managing buttons seems impossible especially when at school, sew velcro onto the shirt and permanently sew the button on the front.

Tying shoelaces is another difficult skill. Velcro straps on shoes have made life much easier for children. Shoelace 'holders' are also available in department stores, shoe-repair shops and some chemists. The following is a method of teaching children how to tie a shoelace. There are other methods, so choose the one that seems the easiest and stick to the same method when teaching the skill.

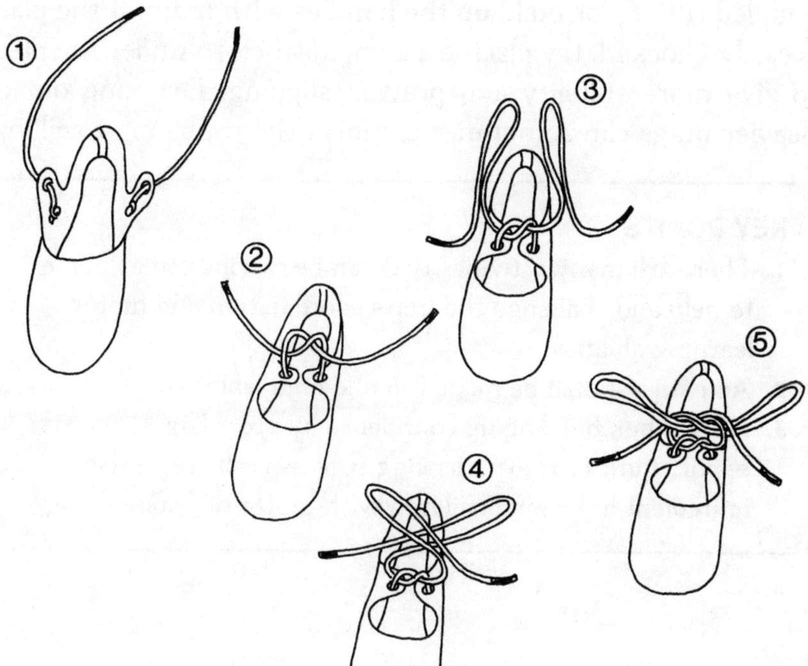

- **Toileting:** some children not only have difficulty with managing fastenings at the toilet but also with wiping themselves properly. Use of velcro instead of buttons or a small loop on a zip can often make management of clothing easier. If wiping is a problem, try wiping from the front while seated on the toilet. Children with poor balance or body awareness find cleaning from behind more difficult while standing.
- **Eating:** using a knife with a serrated edge can often make the cutting of food easier. Even a sharper knife is worth trying. If your child has difficulty grasping cutlery, look for thicker handled cutlery or build up the handles with foam. If the plate is easily knocked, try placing a damp dish-cloth under the plate to give more stability and prevent slipping. Drinking out of heavier mugs can sometimes diminish the problem of spilling.

KEY POINTS

1. There are many activities that can be carried out at home to help and challenge children's coordination and motor learning abilities.
2. Activities should be made fun and enjoyable.
3. Remember, building up confidence by providing opportunities for experiencing success is the essential ingredient in helping children with motor difficulties.

CHAPTER 7

HOBBIES AND HAPPINESS: THE IMPORTANCE OF LEISURE

Leisure is for fun. It is a time when children can discover what they enjoy most and what they can do best. Often, children with motor difficulties find it hard to succeed at leisure activities because so many are orientated around physical and sporting abilities. As parents, we need to find alternative interests that our children can explore, so that they can experience personal satisfaction from leisure pursuits like their more coordinated peers. This chapter looks at those hobbies and activities which do not require a high level of motor proficiency.

CHOOSING APPROPRIATE LEISURE ACTIVITIES

It is easy to force children into a particular leisure activity, believing that it will help improve their gross or fine motor abilities — for example, taking up piano, violin, ballet, tap dancing, athletics or gymnastics. As a parent, you should be guided by your child's own level of enthusiasm. Obviously, if he is keen and interested in the pursuit of such activities, he should be encouraged — as long as no pressure is placed upon him to reach a certain standard in a set time by a far from sympathetic teacher. In other words, your child needs the opportunity to develop these skills at his own pace. It is easy for him to lose the enjoyment and fun in activities, once the priority becomes the perfection of style.

Be guided by your child's own level of enthusiasm when choosing leisure activities.

Sometimes we often hope that playing sports such as soccer or cricket with the other kids or joining 'little athletics' will help our child 'get it altogether'. The reality is, however, that for most children who are clumsy and uncoordinated, participating in competitive sports situations is often a recipe for disaster. These situations only tend to reinforce your child's feelings of failure because he may well be the one who always comes last in the race or drops the ball at the wrong time. Once again, if your child is keen to participate in such activities don't squash or be negative about his enthusiasm. Some children do have a genuine interest in these activities, and their high level of motivation can help override some of the difficulties.

One nine-year-old boy I worked with was not at all well-coordinated, and had difficulties in even the basic self-care skills such as dressing and tying shoelaces. However, he loved playing soccer with his friends and he was accepted because he had a great sense of humour and happy personality. His popularity as a person allowed his team mates to be forgiving of the unfortunate mistakes he made on the soccer field.

As parents you are the ones who know your child best. If, from experience, you know that your child easily gets hurt and upset when participating in organised children's groups, don't feel guilty if you withdraw your child from the organisation. It is easy to be pressured by other parents to enrol children in certain clubs and groups. There is no need to feel you are a non-caring parent if you fail to become involved. Remember, the aim is to explore interests, build up self-esteem and allow your child to be happy. Leisure is for fun, and there are also plenty of fun things to do at home.

SOME IDEAS

The following suggestions are activities which may be more appropriate for children who find it hard to become involved in competitive sports. They are general ideas, which have been collected from parents who have discovered alternative ways of helping their child develop satisfying and rewarding interests.

Bushwalking

Bushwalking and going on picnics is not only enjoyable but strengthens family relationships. It is an opportunity for your child to exercise and be fit, without relying on being proficient in coordination. Through walking in the natural environment, your child has the opportunity to develop additional interests; for example, taking note of the different plants and vegetation, and the birds and rock formations. This early exposure to the natural environment can be the beginning of a life-long interest.

Swimming

Swimming is an excellent activity because it provides your child with the opportunity to exercise, to socialise with other children, and is fun for the whole family. Poorly coordinated children should be encouraged to swim, although the learning process probably will take longer than with other children. The main thing is that the swimming teacher has an awareness of your child's difficulties, and that the teaching methods should be positive and encouraging. The problem with learning free-style swimming, is that children have to do at least three things at once. Remember, once the pressured and 'looking for style' approach is used, your child may lose confidence and interest. The two most important things children need to learn are water safety and how to enjoy the water. Development of a swimming style can come later. Swimming during winter in an indoor heated pool provides opportunity to become confident in water before the summer months arrive.

Fishing

Fishing is another family activity which can be fun, and takes the pressure off children. It is probably easier for your child to fish with a small rod and reel rather than using a hand line because he is less likely to get the line in a tangle, especially if there is a fish on the end. Obviously some help and instruction will initially need to be given when casting. Watching floats bob in the water can have a calming effect on children, and can be especially beneficial for hyperactive children. It may seem strange, but some of the most active children I see actually enjoy fishing, and even just being in a boat will help soothe and settle. If your child seems to have an interest in fishing, buy him magazines to foster the interest and increase his knowledge in the sport.

Computers

Computers are popular with most children and are proving to be of great value for those with motor difficulties. 'Arcade games' that use a joystick encourage eye-hand coordination, as well as helping children focus on what they are doing. Word processing provides a means of alternative written communication for children with motor-based writing difficulties. There are also many educational software packages available, covering a wide range of school related topics. Before you rush out and buy a computer, it is important to check with the class teacher what type of computers the school is using and the appropriateness of buying a particular model.

Starting a Collection

Children often enjoy collecting toys and objects of interest. It need not necessarily be insects and butterflies, but whatever the latest craze is: a series of small toys such as dinosaurs for younger children, or pictures of cars and footy heroes for older children. Children who are very keen on collections frequently link up with children of similar interests, so that comparisons and swapping of items and ideas occurs.

Pets

Most children enjoy pets. Looking after a pet encourages a sense of responsibility and caring, and children love to fuss over a friendly pet. Taking the dog for a walk is excellent exercise for all concerned. However, be warned: before you rush out and buy a dog, bird or fish, be prepared to do the bulk of the caring in the long-run. Children often have the habit of losing interest in the daily care of pets, by becoming preoccupied with another or new interest.

Cooking

Interest in cooking can be achieved if the process does not take too long, and the results are quick and enjoyable to eat. Making pop-corn, chocolate crackles, pikelets, and sprinkling favourite ingredients on pizzas are favourites. Alternatively, let your child develop his own creativity in cooking; this is how the world's greatest chefs develop their talents. Everyone enjoys eating and successful cooks are praised, so being involved in cooking is another way of building up your child's confidence and encouraging a sense of achievement. As adults, we may consider cooking a bit of a chore. However, this is an activity which can easily be made enjoyable for our children.

Drama Groups

Participation in drama groups is a very social experience and can be lots of fun. It provides your child with the opportunity to express feelings and emotions, as well as encouraging communication skills. I once knew a fourteen-year-old boy who had major difficulties with concentration and writing. He had a keen interest in poetry and short stories, as well as a great sense of humour. His parents recognised his interests and so encouraged him to join the local theatrical group. It was discovered that he had considerable talent in acting, and it was not long before he was playing leading roles.

Music

Music provides many avenues for children to develop talents and interests. Some instruments require more fine manipulative movements than others, for example the piano and string instruments compared to some brass and wind instruments. If your child shows interest in music, he should be encouraged to pursue that interest. The recorder is always a good starting point because it is not a difficult instrument to learn, and provides children with the opportunity to play in groups.

One child I knew had a desire to learn to play the drums. His parents bought him an inexpensive set and he had regular lessons. They found it helped his coordination and gave him a great deal of personal satisfaction. So, if you are brave, drums are another possibility! However, once again be warned: many children may start off with great enthusiasm, but sometimes it does not take long before the enthusiasm fades away. Also, remember that any badly played instrument is not good for parents' nerves! If your child seems to be able to sing in tune and enjoys singing, auditioning for a children's choir is worth considering — not only for the pleasure of singing but also for the social contact with other children of similar musical interests. Children however do not necessarily need to learn to play instruments or sing to gain satisfaction from music. Music appreciation and pleasure can also be achieved through listening to recordings, tapes and building up a collection of 'favourites'.

Horse riding

Horse riding gives your child the opportunity to practise balancing skills, body awareness and increase his strength. It also helps him to develop a sense of right and left as he learns to control and guide the horse. There are opportunities both in the city and certainly in the country to expose children to riding lessons and trail rides.

Gardening

A number of children enjoy planting seeds, and take an interest in the way flowers, vegetables and other plants grow. An interest in gardening can be encouraged by cultivating plants which produce results quickly. For example, radishes, zucchinis, beans and mushrooms can easily be cultivated in boxes available from nurseries.

Excursions to Sporting Events

Taking an interest in major sporting events and going to matches and grand finals with Dad keeps your child in touch with what is happening in the world of sport. Knowing match results and the names of sport celebrities provides the opportunity to join in conversation and contribute knowledgeably with peers. This may help lessen your child's sense of being on the 'outer' when sporting interests and achievements are being discussed.

Photography

Photography can be encouraged from an early age. Nonexpensive cameras are able to produce good results, which give pleasure and enjoyment to both the photographer and subject. Children enjoy taking photos of their friends, family and special events. As the development of photographs is quick these days, it does not take long before the results can be seen. It is probably a good idea to buy film with the least number of exposures, so your child does not have to wait too long for the film to be finished before developing. Older children may learn how to develop a print either at home or in a club. Watching black and white images appear before your eyes is a real thrill.

KEY POINTS

1. Leisure activities provide opportunities for clumsy and poorly coordinated children to discover their interests and talents.
2. Often unintentionally, involvement in competitive sports sets these children up to fail which does little to help self-esteem.
3. Leisure activities should be fun, and should not be forced on uninterested children in the belief that a particular activity will help their clumsiness and poor coordination.
4. There are many alternative interests that children can be encouraged to pursue that do not rely on a high level of motor competence. When trying to come up with ideas on suitable leisure pursuits, be guided by the games and activities to which your child naturally gravitates.

CHAPTER 8

SKIPPING OR TRIPPING: WHAT'S THE NEXT STEP?

It is only in recent years that we have realised how difficult life can be for children who are clumsy and uncoordinated. These children, despite the diversity of their difficulties, are now recognised as an identifiable group whose problems should not be dismissed lightly. In this chapter two important issues about future progress are discussed.

WHAT IMPROVEMENTS CAN I EXPECT?

Real and positive gains can be experienced by your child if her motor difficulties are identified and encouragement given. Opportunities to practise and develop problem areas in an understanding and caring environment are the key to helping children with coordination problems. We need to realise, however, that practice even over a long time does not eventually turn a clumsy and uncoordinated child into the school's champion athlete or a graceful ballet dancer. These children, as with all of us, can improve their motor coordination with practice. However, we all can only improve to the level of our in-built capabilities no matter how hard we try.

We know that it is very difficult to perfect any motor skill when there is pressure placed on us to reach certain expectations. Both children and adults can easily lose heart if unable to keep up with others. It is even more difficult when we are in a group and can see that we are falling behind everyone else. It would be interesting to know why some adults drop out of aerobics classes. No doubt one major reason is because they find it difficult to keep up with the pace and standard of the rest of the class. Children cannot drop out of situations which they find uncomfortable as easily as adults. If your child is pushed too hard to achieve success in areas which are difficult, she may totally refuse to even attempt the task. This can flow on to a pattern of stubbornness and refusal in many aspects of her daily life.

The flow-on effect can work both ways. Restored self-confidence can also influence many aspects of your child's life, not just the motor skills themselves. Encouraging hobbies, interests and therapy, if needed, are ways that you can help your child experience success. When children are given opportunities to feel good about themselves, they are more willing to try new and more challenging tasks because a new self-assurance has been fostered.

DO CLUMSY AND UNCOORDINATED CHILDREN GROW OUT OF IT?

As children pass from childhood to adolescence, the difficulties encountered in the earlier years tend to diminish as their motor system matures. However, for some children, some of the difficulties may linger if the clumsiness and poor coordination is significant during childhood. Handwriting difficulties in particular may persist into adulthood. Fortunately, we live in an age of word processing and people with handwriting difficulties now have alternative means to communicate legibly. Remember, in the long run it is the content of writing that is important, not the style or neatness.

We live in a society where there is a great deal of emphasis placed on sporting and physical abilities. Even in the preschool years, too much emphasis can be placed on gross motor skills. No doubt you have met parents who think that because their child runs, climbs, skips and jumps well, they must be brilliant in all areas of their development. No doubt there are academics and university professors whose coordination abilities are not their strengths.

I am sure we all have friends who are a bit clumsy, uncoordinated and generally 'accident prone'. These are the people you keep away from your best crystal glassware! We know they can still have fun lives because most adults focus on the activities they are good at. This can include many non-competitive sporting activities which do not rely on a high level of motor planning and coordination ability, such as surfing, swimming, fishing, bushwalking and jogging.

It is therefore important to be reminded that the pursuit of enjoyable leisure activities is of great value in the long run. As parents, we should try and seek out areas of success for our children, instead of always keeping a narrow focus on the difficulties. The difficulties certainly should not be dismissed. However, we need to keep a broad and balanced view. Our children must never grow up being allowed to feel that they are not much good at anything. Childhood should hold memories of enjoyable and fun experiences, not memories of struggling, trying to keep up with others and being constantly reminded of the difficulties. Emphasis on success, fun, hobbies, interests and family times is the balanced and positive approach which I believe is necessary to help children who seem clumsy and uncoordinated in motor skills. In other words, we want our children to go through life 'skipping not tripping'!

KEY POINTS

1. It is only in recent years that the problems facing clumsy and uncoordinated children have been recognised.
2. By recognising coordination difficulties and boosting confidence, our children should emerge socially and emotionally much stronger.
3. The outlook is positive, with a bit of help through the school years when motor abilities seem unnecessarily important.

APPENDIX I

CONCENTRATION DIFFICULTIES: ATTENTION DEFICIT DISORDER

Many children referred to me because of poor coordination skills, also have difficulties in concentration. Associated with concentration problems, is an increased incidence of specific learning difficulties; for example, poor reading, writing and spelling (dyslexia). This means that for many children, their problems are not just the learning of motor skills but also some aspects of school work. Their behaviour can also be difficult at times.

Attention Deficit Disorder (ADD) is the medical term which describes children with problems in concentration. All children at some stage in the school day have lapses in concentration. However, for some children, the in-built difficulties in concentration can be so constant that they impair the child's ability to learn both in and out of the classroom. The combination of inattention, over-activity and certain associated behaviours, is what used to be termed 'hyperactivity'. The modern medical term is Attention Deficit Hyperactivity Disorder (ADHD).

ADD and ADHD are imprecise descriptive terms which focus on the most significant feature, that is, the inability to concentrate. Other associated behaviours include impulsiveness, acting first without thinking, restlessness, a low frustration level and poor self-esteem. More boys than girls who are referred to therapy seem to have difficulties in concentration. A number of parents also report that they had similar difficulties when they were children.

Children who lack concentration can be very frustrating to teach, and even more difficult to live with. They don't seem to listen to what is being said and act as if instructions go through one ear and out the other. So confusing is this, that many children I see have already had their hearing tested as parents suspect a hearing loss.

Poor concentration is a particular problem at school, where children can be distracted by any movement, the sound of a pencil dropping or others talking. Children with this problem are impulsive, and frequently act before they think, which can lead them into troublesome situations. These children may talk when they should be quiet, act the clown, leave their chair and be disruptive in the class. They often go on about anything in their conversation, and interrupt their parents because they find it hard to wait their turn to talk.

Many children with poor concentration are restless and fidgety which is why the term 'hyperactivity' was used. When seated at their school desk they wriggle, swing their legs back and forth under the chair and continually look around.

At home, many parents find life very difficult. These children can be constantly demanding. They easily get 'bored' and find it hard to settle into any one activity for a meaningful length of time, and often want new and different things to do during the day. Once their requests are granted, they easily lose interest and are rarely satisfied.

Many of these children are somewhat disorganised. They leave schoolwork behind, forget to take their gym shoes or lunch box to school, or alternatively forget to bring them home. They are messy and seem oblivious to the trail of destruction and debris they leave behind them. They can also get easily over-excited and 'out of control'. Socially, they often act silly in a group with their mates, and they can become bossy and difficult when playing with one friend.

Other children may not be over-active, but still experience difficulties in concentration. These are the daydreamers. They tend to sit quietly in the classroom, distracted by their own thoughts which may have been related to what was said initially but somehow, during the process of listening, the relevant thoughts seem to 'float away'. These children cause no trouble at school, they are just hard to teach and fail quietly.

MANAGEMENT

Paediatricians, teachers, psychologists and therapists are the professionals most frequently involved in helping these children. The following approaches are those most commonly used.

Behaviour Management

These children respond well to structure and routine in their daily lives. It is helpful if their week consists of activities which are regular and programed. They function best if their lives are organised. Outdoor activities are important, especially when they return from a day confined in the classroom. After school, they need to burn off excess energy.

These children respond best to discipline which is consistent. By discipline, I do not mean yelling or screaming at a child. This approach tends to stir them up more. It is important to aim for peace where possible and avoid confrontational situations. 'Time out' is one of the best ways for everyone to 'cool off'. The message is clear and simple: 'Go to your room to calm down'. It is important to make it clear to your child, just what behaviours are unacceptable, and use 'time out' sparingly. If it is used for every annoying incident, a child could end up in their room all day! Don't over-discipline; use 'time out' methods for when they are needed.

These children need their self-esteem boosted, so the good things that they do should be noticed and given lots of praise. It's easy to get drawn into focusing on everything that is bad. Watch for good things and acknowledge them no matter how trivial they may seem. The idea is to encourage and reward the good behaviour and hope it is repeated. Where possible, try and ignore the negative behaviour.

If you are having difficulty achieving appropriate behavioural techniques with your child, the most appropriate professionals to seek advice from are psychologists.

Teaching Strategies

If children are experiencing difficulties with school work, it is important to first discuss concerns with the class teacher. If they are worried, they will arrange an appointment with the school counsellor who is a psychologist attached to almost every school. When Attention Deficit is a problem, a simple strategy such as sitting a child near the front of the class is one way of helping. More direct encouragement in one-to-one teaching with structured steps, or a remedial teaching program, may also be needed. If in doubt, discuss your worries with the school.

Medication

Is sometimes needed if none of the above strategies appear

to be helping. Ritalin and Dexamphetamine are the most commonly prescribed drugs to help children with major concentration difficulties and hyperactivity. The staff I work with regard these medications as safe, and useful in a significant number of cases, particularly when used in conjunction with the above strategies. These drugs are called stimulant medications and they enable children to focus selectively on a task. They act, not as sedatives, but to help the child focus his natural concentration abilities and keep his mind on the task. The problem of being distracted by extraneous sights and sounds, as well as their own thoughts, can be reduced. Once this occurs, these children are in a better position to listen to and follow the teacher's lessons. At home, children are able to be more 'focused' on doing one thing at a time, rather than rushing through the house like a whirlwind, being easily excited and impulsive. When impulsiveness is reduced, children are able to think before they upset others and, more importantly, they are able to think before placing themselves in dangerous situations.

Parents obviously have concerns about using medication for concentration difficulties. It is therefore important for you to be well-informed about the use of such medications before making a decision regarding their appropriateness. This information is best provided by a paediatrician.

Diet

Removal of certain foods (mostly those containing artificial colourings and preservatives as well as some natural foods) from a child's diet has been observed to reduce hyperactivity in some children but not all.

Parents may recognise what foods upset their child, and

subsequently try and steer clear of them. Restricting foods containing artificial colourings and flavourings will not harm your child nutritionally. However, if fruits, vegetables and other staple foods seem to upset a child, care should be taken not to inappropriately eliminate these foods which are important to a healthy and well-balanced diet. Diets are not much fun for any of us, so it is important to find out if a diet eliminating natural foods is necessary. Dieticians are the best professionals to consult if further advice and assessment is needed.

In conclusion, the management of concentration difficulties and hyperactivity requires the involvement of several professionals. The main people involved are psychologists, remedial teachers, paediatricians, therapists and dietitians.

The fact that several professionals are involved indicates that there are no simple solutions for helping these children. However, when each aspect is considered and the various approaches used in conjunction with each other, a great deal can be offered to help these children and their families. The reality is that life can be very difficult living with an Attention Deficit/Hyperactive child, and parents should not feel hesitant in seeking professional advice and support.

THE HYPERACTIVE CHILD

From Toddler Taming, *copyright © Dr Christopher Green, 1990, published by Doubleday, Australia.*

Symptoms of hyperactivity (Attention Deficit Hyperactivity Disorder)

The older hyperactive child may have many but not necessarily all of the following symptoms:

Poor attention

- *a poor listener, forgets instructions, lists or messages, is easily distracted*
- *visually inattentive, blind to changes, skips paragraphs when reading, blind to oncoming hazards*
- *absorbed in own thoughts, a dreamer, spaced out*

Impulsive

- *leaps before he looks, mouth is in motion before mind is in gear, hits before he thinks and is consequently often branded as aggressive, easily led*

Never satisfied

- *interrogates parents mercilessly, gets stuck on one idea, gets a reward and immediately wants more, doesn't learn easily from experience*

Overactive

- *irritable baby, likes to be on the move*
- *overactive toddler, almost motor-driven*
- *fidgety, disruptive, easily distracted schoolchild*
- *prefers to be outside, worse with noise, tension or crowds*

Variable performance

- *behaviour fluctuates from day to day, some days does well at school, on others might just as well have stayed at home*

Disorganisation

- *right/left confusion*
- *late in learning to tie shoelaces, puts clothes on back to front, messy eater, poor flow of movement, finds it hard to perform two actions at same time, messy, finds it difficult to do things in sequence*

Social handicap

- *wants to mix as an equal but can't bring this about, speaks without thinking, a poor loser, low tolerance of failure, will act silly to gain attention in a group*

Clumsiness

- *is particularly clumsy*
- *impulsiveness causes accidents*

Poor self-esteem

- *probably present early on, exacerbated by social and academic failure*

Language problems

- *forgets what he's saying in mid-sentence*
- *interrupts others due to impulsiveness and fear of forgetting*
- *gets confused over yesterday/tomorrow, earlier/later, etc*

Others

- *specific learning problems: probably half will have some degree of weakness, for example, reading, spelling, maths, etc*
- *sleep problems: can find it hard to settle at night and will be a restless sleeper*
- *touchy, rarely satisfied, irritating yet very sensitive*

APPENDIX II

KEEPING CHILDREN (AND PARENTS) ENTHUSIASTIC: SOME TIPS

When you find time to set aside to work with your child on areas of difficulty, the following suggestions may help you to keep your child motivated and interested. It is easy to lose heart if specific remedial activities seem difficult — it is hard to keep up a momentum of enthusiasm. Here are some tips:

1. Choose times when your child and you are reasonably relaxed. This may be after dinner, bathtime or on weekends. Straight after school is not a good time, as children need to unwind and you no doubt are busy preparing the dinner. Parents also need to unwind after a busy day, so watching that favourite television program is all part of the process.
2. Set aside time which you know is realistic for your routine and your child's concentration span. It may be ten, twenty minutes or even half an hour. You are the best judge of an appropriate time frame.
3. Start off and finish with those activities at which you know your child will succeed. The initial activity should catch your child's interest, while the last one should end on a good note. In between the successful activities do the more demanding tasks.
4. Encourage your child to choose an activity which they particularly enjoy — this activity can be the 'motivator' which can precede the more challenging games.
5. Children love taking turns. I find this a most useful way

to help keep children interested. For example, if you want a child to copy a pattern while threading beads, take turns to complete the activity. It is fun for children to spot adults' mistakes — so make mistakes on purpose.

6. Use rewards such as ticks, stickers, stars or even just a big hug when you can see your child is really trying.

7. Use your own voice and facial expression to give the message that you are pleased, enthusiastic, etc. Enthusiasm is contagious. If you cannot maintain the momentum, finish the set time on an enjoyable activity and leave it at that.

8. Include the other children in the family, because a group can make the suggested games and activities more fun. It also avoids the others feeling excluded.

9. Vary the activities as much as possible to maintain interest.

10. Remember, guilt is a great dampener to enthusiasm. Never feel guilty if you think you are not spending enough time with your child. You are probably giving more helpful, positive messages to build up confidence than you realise.

APPENDIX III

GETTING IN TOUCH WITH SERVICES

Occupational therapists, physiotherapists and speech pathologists are usually located in the following areas:
Public Hospitals: listed in the phone book under 'Hospitals'. Ask if the departments employ therapists who specialise in seeing children.
Community Health Centres/Child Health Centres: listed in the phone book under 'Community' or 'Child'. Most of these centres also have access to doctors, psychologists, social workers, community nurses, audiologists, orthoptists and dietitians.
Private Practice: for information on paediatric therapists in private practice, the state associations for each profession are able to provide this information.

ORGANISATIONS TO HELP CHILDREN WITH LEARNING DIFFICULTIES

SPELD (Specific Learning Difficulties Association): Is an association of parents and professionals involved in helping children and adults with learning difficulties. They provide information to parents through a counselling service, newsletter, library and seminars. There is a branch of SPELD in every state:
SPELD NSW INC, 129 Greenwich Road, Greenwich 2065. Ph: 02 906 2977

SPELD VICTORIA INC, 494 Brunswick Street, Fitzroy Vic 3065. Ph: (03) 489 4344
SPELD QLD INC, 21 Edmondstone Street, South Brisbane Qld 4101. Ph: (07) 844 6868
SPELD SA INC, 298 Portrush Road, Kensington SA 5068. Ph: (08) 31 1655
DYSLEXIA-SPELD FOUNDATION WA INC, PO Box 409, South Perth WA 6951. Ph: (09) 367 3494
SPELD ACT INC, c/- Shout Office, PO Box 717, Mawson ACT 2607. Ph: (06) 290 1984
SPELD TASMANIA, PO Box 154, North Hobart Tas 7002. Ph: (002) 44 5172

ACLD (Association for Children with Learning Disabilities): This organisation provides remedial teaching, an early education program, educational counselling, occupational and physiotherapy, recreational programs and a library service. It is based only in Sydney (Pindari Centre (ACLD Inc.), 12-14 Pindari Road, Peakhurst South NSW 2210. Ph: 02 534 1710).

BIBLIOGRAPHY

Arnheim, D. & Sinclair, W., *The Clumsy Child: A Program of Motor Therapy,* The C. V. Mosby Company, St. Louis, 1979.

Bonney, M. & Perks, J., *Difficulty with Handwriting?: A Handbook of Ideas and Remediation,* Therapy Resource Team, Chatswood Child and Family Health, Sydney, 1989.

Coley, I., *Paediatric Assessment of Self Care Activities,* The C. V. Mosby Company, St. Louis, 1978.

Corkille Briggs, D., *Your Child's Self Esteem,* Dolphin Books, Doubleday & Company Inc., New York, 1975.

Fink, B., *Sensory Motor Integration Activities,* Arizona Therapy Skills Builders: Division of Communication Skills Builders, Arizona, 1989.

Gallahue, D., *Motor Development and Movement Experience for Young Children (3–7),* John Wiley & Sons, New York, 1976.

— *Understanding Motor Development in Children,* John Wiley & Sons, New York, 1982.

Gesell, A., Ilg, F. & Ames, L., *The Child From Five to Ten,* Revised edition, Harper & Row, New York, 1977.

Gordon, N. & McKinlay, I. (eds), *Helping Clumsy Children,* Churchill Livingston, London, 1980.

Green C., *Toddler Taming: A Guide for Your Child from One to Four,* Doubleday, Australia, 1990.

Gubbay, S., *The Clumsy Child: A Study of Developmental Apraxia and Agnostic Ataxia,* W. B. Saunders Co. Ltd, London, 1975.

Hornsby, B., *Overcoming Dyslexia: A Straightforward Guide for Parents and Teachers,* Martin Dunitz Ltd, London, 1989.

Laszlo, J. & Bairstow, P., *Perceptual Motor Behaviour: Developmental Assessment and Therapy,* Holt, Rinehart & Winston Ltd, London, 1985.

Mulvaney, A., *Look Who's Talking: How to Help Children with Their Communication Skills,* Simon & Schuster Australia, Sydney, 1991.

Pheloung, B., *Help Your Child to Learn,* Revised edition, Bantam/ Tortoiseshell Press Book, Australia, 1988.

Rostain, A., 'Attention Deficit Disorder in Children and Adolescents', *Paediatric Clinics of North America,* vol. 30, No 3, June 1991.

Serfontein, G., *The Hidden Handicap: How to Help Children Who Suffer from Dyslexia, Hyperactivity and Learning Difficulties,* Simon & Schuster Australia, Sydney, 1990.

Sheridan, M., *Children's Developmental Progress,* NFER Publishing Co., U.K., 1973.

INDEX